No Strings

*Untangling Your Heart's
Attachment To Money*

No Strings:
Untangling Your Heart's Attachment to Money

Copyright © 2016 by Grafted Life Ministries (Grafted Life).

All rights reserved. Printed in the United States of America. No part of this book may be used or reproduced in any manner whatsoever without written permission except in the case of brief quotations embodied in critical articles and reviews.

Unless otherwise indicated, all Scripture quotations are from the ESV® Bible (The Holy Bible, English Standard Version®), copyright © 2001 by Crossway, a publishing ministry of Good News Publishers. Used by permission. All rights reserved.

Scripture quotations marked (NLT) are taken from the Holy Bible, New Living Translation, copyright ©1996, 2004, 2007, 2013, 2015 by Tyndale House Foundation. Used by permission of Tyndale House Publishers, Inc., Carol Stream, Illinois 60188. All rights reserved.

Published by Grafted Life Ministries (Grafted Life).

For more information about the ministries of Grafted Life, visit our website at www.graftedlife.org

Design by Ryan Swindoll
Audio by Landon Swindoll

Special thanks to Jody Humber for his support on this project.

Edition 1, May 2016

ISBN-10: 1532796862
ISBN-13: 978-1532796869

Contents

Introduction 5

Week 1: Getting Started 13

Week 2: Seeking Financial Freedom 19

Week 3: God Is A Giver 29

Week 4: Acknowledging Our History With Money 41

Week 5: Our History With God And Money 53

Week 6: What Is Our Current Identity? 67

Week 7: Using Money To Create A Reputation 79

Week 8: In God We Trust 91

Week 9: Trusting God Together 101

Week 10: Contentment: A Sign Of Freedom 113

Week 11: Free To Choose 125

Week 12: Free To Partner With God 137

Going On From Here 151

Reflections For Christians in Leadership 163

About Grafted Life 177

Introduction

For the love of money is a root of all kinds of evils. It is through this craving that some have wandered away from the faith and pierced themselves with many pangs.

1 Timothy 6:10

Welcome to *No Strings: Untangling Your Heart's Attachment To Money*. While Jesus was on earth, He often used the subject of money as an illustration to open people's hearts to His instruction about the Kingdom of God. Jesus' teachings point us to this truth: it is easy for us to become attached to our possessions. Money represents a significant temptation in our lives—to depend on it for our survival and success, to use it to promote our comfort or reputation. Money is a powerful adversary to our relationships with God and others, whether we have a little of it or a lot.

Because of money's influence, there are numerous ways that we try to control our attraction to it. We can set up financial structures that put boundaries on the way that we spend, save or give our money away. We can seek the help of financial institutions or advisors to make wise money decisions. But as good as these external options are, unless we are willing to look internally

> » at the way our resources affect our emotions,
> » at what motivates our spending decisions,
> » at the underlying meaning that we attach to the assets that we possess or desire,

then we have not explored all that Jesus wants us to evaluate. If we desire lasting change and true freedom, we need to look at the deeper issues of our hearts.

So, how can we untangle the strings of our hearts that may be attached to our money or possessions? What is the process to becoming someone who is free financially? How can we interact with God and others as we explore the meaning of money in our lives?

In the next few months, *No Strings* will lead you on an interactive journey to explore these questions with God and your Christian community. Alongside the opportunity to learn what Scripture teaches about possessions, you will have the opportunity to evaluate your personal finances and your heart's reaction to your current resources. The exercises and reflections will invite open, honest and real conversations with yourself and God about what really matters to you regarding money.

Sound intriguing? If so, keep reading to learn all you need to know to get the most out of each week. Because this study is likely different from previous ones that you have participated in, the orientation that follows is important. It will help you get your bearings going forward.

Blessings to you as you begin. Our prayers have gone before you and we know that God goes with you. May you feel His loving presence as your companion throughout every step of the journey.

Orientation

In order to get you started on the right foot, we offer these seven concepts to orient you to the type of study you are participating in. Take some time before you begin to reflect on these points. But also keep them in mind as you proceed. It may be helpful to review this page if somewhere along the journey you find yourself wondering about any of the reflective questions or activities in the study.

No Strings focuses on biblical concepts.

This study begins with Scripture. Each week you will find a set of verses that ground the Lesson for that session. All of the remaining activities are meant to guide you to reflect on the meaning of the biblical ideas and to apply them in your daily life.

***No Strings* is interactive.**
This study will involve more than just reading, answering and discussing some questions. You will be asked to engage in a comprehensive process towards personal and spiritual growth. From listening to podcast teachings to interacting with your financial resources, you will be invited to learn and practice core biblical principles in ways that truly impact your heart and your life.

***No Strings* includes God in the process.**
This study emphasizes times of prayer. As you participate in the activities and reflections, you will be asked to talk to God about what you are doing. These conversations are meant to deepen your awareness that God is with you all the time and to strengthen your ability to connect with Him in daily life.

***No Strings* encourages you to think.**
This study includes many opportunities for you to record your thoughts about the biblical concepts, your financial situation and the activities that you engage in. Though sometimes the questions may seem similar to previous ones that you have answered, each one is designed to expand your perspective and reveal your understanding of the weekly ideas.

***No Strings* asks you to explore your feelings.**
This study poses many questions that focus your attention on your emotional responses. This is done very purposefully. Regardless of our gender, our feelings influence the financial decisions that we make and can lead us to understand the motivations of our hearts. Because of their importance, the reflection questions will often ask you to evaluate what you are feeling. This practice helps you to grow in awareness of your emotional responses and gives you an opportunity to talk openly with God about the state of your heart.

***No Strings* flexes with your schedule.**
This study is set up in a 12 week format with an approximate 2 or 3 hour time commitment each week to complete all of the activities. However, you should feel the freedom to alter the pace of how you engage with the materials. Although we do not recommend that you go faster than one lesson per week, you might desire to slow the process down in order to get the most out of the activities and times of reflection. Allow

yourself the time to let the concepts sink in and to participate in the Real Life Practices. This journey is not designed to be a speed race, but rather a leisurely walk with God and some fellow Christians.

No Strings works.

This study includes proven practices that open people's hearts and lives to be changed by the Holy Spirit. But these activities only work if you engage. The practices will require effort on your part. Sustaining that effort may not always be easy. At times, some activities will seem uncomfortable, challenging or maybe even pointless. Some questions might press you, and you may feel resistant to engage fully with what is being suggested to you.

Pay attention when this happens. Rather than force yourself to move on, we suggest that you take some time to talk with God about what you are feeling and to ask for His help in completing what you can. Remember that there is nothing magical about the practices in this study, but there is great potential for change when we turn our hearts toward God. The ultimate work of this study and the point of each activity is growth in our relationship with Him.

The Activities

No Strings includes five different weekly activities.

The Lesson

The audio podcast begins the activities for each session. Each Lesson podcast focuses on the Scripture for the week, offering opportunities to listen to the verses and to consider application of the biblical concepts in your relationship with money, God and others. Each recording is about 15 minutes long and can be accessed on the Grafted Life website.

It is easy to stream or download the podcasts. Just follow these simple steps.

1. Go to www.graftedlife.org on your computer or mobile device and log in with an existing account or register a new account. You can create a free account using the "Member Login" menu on the main navigation bar.

2. From the account dashboard, click to "Add Online Content."

3. Input the following case-sensitive code: AT2NFDKG

4. Select the podcasts for *No Strings*. You can stream the podcasts online or download the podcasts for listening on the audio player of your choice.

5. Bookmark www.graftedlife.org/podcasts for quick access.

Note: For those who have difficulty hearing or prefer to read along, we have PDF transcripts of the Lessons available on our website on the podcast page at no additional charge. Follow the instructions above to access the transcripts.

The Real Life Practice

After you have listened to the Lesson, you will be invited to practice the scriptural concepts in your life. These activities are designed to help you engage with and process your current financial realities. This book guides you through the process of completing each exercise.

Participating in these practices allows you to experience how your heart is potentially attached to money or possessions rather than to God. They help you to see where growth is needed and where small changes can make a big difference in the way you relate to your resources.

> *If you experience any thoughts or feelings during a Real Life Practice that you find concerning or overwhelming, we recommend that you talk about it with a pastor, counselor, spiritual director, or trusted friend.*

Observation Notes

After you have completed the Real Life Practice, you will be led through a short series of questions that help you observe what happened in the practice. These opportunities for evaluation are needed because while we are engaging in exercises, our minds are occupied in the task. When we take time later to turn our full attention to what happened, we have an increased ability to see the whole picture, evaluate our emotional responses, and expand our perspective. This also gives us an opportunity to include God in the process, asking that His perspective be added to our own insight about the experience.

Reflection

To complete your personal exercises for the session, you will answer a series of reflective questions designed to integrate the components of the study for that week. These questions give you an opportunity to revisit the Scripture verses and the Lesson in light of the Real Life Practice, and to consider your own thoughts and feeling about the material. This ending evaluation allows you to think about what has been beneficial and what you would like to apply going forward.

This time of reflection is also a time of prayer—a time to talk over your thoughts and feelings with God. He will be there to direct your thoughts as you open your heart and mind to what He wants to communicate.

The Group Discussion

At the end of each session, you will find questions for group discussion. These conversation starters are designed to help a group share their experiences with each other. Having the opportunity to verbally process what happened in your personal reflection and to synthesize the activities can bring clarity to what God is doing in our hearts and lives. Participating in the group discussion also gives you an opportunity to learn from other people's stories and perspectives.

If you are not participating in *No Strings* as a part of a small group, we recommend that you invite one or two other people to do the study with you. Going through the process with others adds a helpful dimension to the study experience.

REFLECTIONS FOR CHRISTIANS IN LEADERSHIP

If you hold a position of leadership within a church, non-profit, or business, we have provided additional thought-provoking questions for you in the Appendix of this book. These opportunities for reflection guide you to consider and converse with God about your responsibilities as a steward of others' resources.

As you go through the weeks of this study, pondering your personal attachment to money, the leadership questions correlate with and supplement the themes of each session helping you to prayerfully consider how your attachments influence your organizational decisions as well. We recommend that you use them for personal edification and as possible group discussion opportunities with others on your leadership team.

> To help you get started with these questions, listen to the podcast "A Message for Leaders" on our website.

WEEK 1
Getting Started

And [Jesus] said to him, "You shall love the Lord your God with all your heart and with all your soul and with all your mind. This is the great and first commandment. And a second is like it: You shall love your neighbor as yourself. On these two commandments depend all the Law and the Prophets."
Matthew 22:37-40

The Lesson   15 minutes

Listen to the podcast for Week 1, accessible at graftedlife.org. You will find instructions on how to access the podcasts on page 8 of the introduction.

This Lesson introduces you to the context of *No Strings* and gives you an idea of what to expect as you participate. Each weekly activity is outlined and described, and helpful tips are offered for getting the most out of this unique study.

Reflection   15-20 minutes

Find a quiet place to consider the questions below. Begin by reading the Scripture verses for this week.

> *And [Jesus] said to him, "You shall love the Lord your God with all your heart and with all your soul and with all your mind. This is the great and first commandment. And a second is like it: You shall love your neighbor as yourself. On these two commandments depend all the Law and the Prophets."*
>
> *Matthew 22:37-40*

✐ What thoughts and feelings do you experience as you read these commandments of Jesus, particularly in light of beginning this course?

✐ What brought you to this study? What are you hoping to get out of it?

Participation in *No Strings* will require a time commitment each week:
- *Listening to the Lesson podcast – 15 minutes*
- *Doing the Real Life Practice – 20 to 40 minutes*
- *Writing Observation Notes – 5 to 10 minutes*
- *Answering Reflection questions – 15 to 30 minutes*
- *Sharing in the Group Discussion – 30 to 60 minutes*

✎ Are you willing and able to set aside time for these activities for each week of the study? What practical changes to your schedule might you need to make in order to fully participate?

✎ As noted in the Lesson, God might use this study to reveal things about yourself and your attachments to money that you did not know. What's your reaction to this thought?

✎ Our relationship to money can also affect our relationships with others, including God. How do you feel about that idea? Does it discourage you or encourage you as you begin this study?

- What do you anticipate will be your greatest obstacle to engaging fully in *No Strings?*

- What do you hope could be the greatest benefit of your participation?

- In light of your answers above, can you offer yourself to God and accept whatever experience He may choose to give you through this study? What would you like to say to Him?

- How has listening to the Lesson and working through the Reflection deepened your understanding of this week's Scripture passage?

Group Discussion   30-60 minutes

Use the questions below to guide your group discussion. This week, we focused on preparing for this study. We also considered Jesus' commandments in Matthew 22:37-40. Refer to your experience with the Lesson and Reflection as you share together.

Read Matthew 22:37-40 aloud.

» From the Scripture passage, what did you discover about your current relationships with God, others and yourself?

» What did you discover about yourself as you considered what it will mean to begin this study?

» How would you like this course to affect your relationship to money? What do you hope to learn?

» What are you expecting or hoping to get out of the group discussions?

» What are you anticipating will be most difficult for you as you engage in the activities and exercises?

» What would you like to ask God for as you commit yourself and your time to *No Strings?*

End the discussion with prayer.

Week 2
Seeking Financial Freedom

"No one can serve two masters, for either he will hate the one and love the other, or he will be devoted to the one and despise the other. You cannot serve God and money."

Matthew 6:24

The Lesson   15 minutes

Listen to the podcast for Week 2. It examines the guiding Scripture passages for *No Strings* and how our hearts' attachment to money can get in the way of our relationship with God.

Real Life Practice   30-60+ minutes

Follow the instructions below to make a non-judgmental survey of the earthly treasures that you possess.

> *As you engage in this exercise, you may feel uncomfortable with what you discover and be tempted to make changes. Keep yourself from acting on those thoughts and feelings. Just make note of them. Then gently direct your attention back to completing the exercise.*

Read our focus verses for this week:

> *Do not lay up for yourselves treasures on earth, where moth and rust destroy and where thieves break in and steal, but lay up for yourselves treasures in heaven, where neither moth nor rust destroys and where thieves do not break in and steal. For where your treasure is, there your heart will be also.*
>
> *No one can serve two masters, for either he will hate the one and love the other, or he will be devoted to the one and despise the other. You cannot serve God and money.*
>
> Matthew 6:19-21 & 24

Financial Survey

> *This exercise is meant to give you a general overview of your financial possessions. Aim to create a basic sketch of your current circumstances. Don't spend too much time trying to be exact or overly thorough.*

- Examine your overall financial situation. What money have you stored up? Look over your records and estimate overall what is in your checking, savings, investments, retirement accounts, etc. Be sure to include any currency you keep on hand. Also note how much debt you owe. (This is just for your awareness. You won't have to share this information with anyone.) Altogether, consider the general amount of money you have. Are you satisfied with what you have, or are you concerned that you have too little or too much?

- Write down any major items that you own, such as, property, modes of transportation, businesses, recreational equipment, etc. Consider the value of the major items that you own. Do you wish you had more, wish you had less or are you content with what you have?

🖉 Walk around your house/apartment/etc. and consider what possessions you have. Open up drawers, cupboards and closets. Simply notice what you see and your reactions to it. If you have any additional items out of sight, such as in an attic, shed, garage or storage unit, try to include those in your observation as well. Consider the amount of items you have. Would you say that you have a lot, an average amount or not enough?

Observation Notes   5-10 minutes

Spend a few minutes answering the following questions based on your experiences with the Real Life Practice.

Refer to the word chart below when answering.

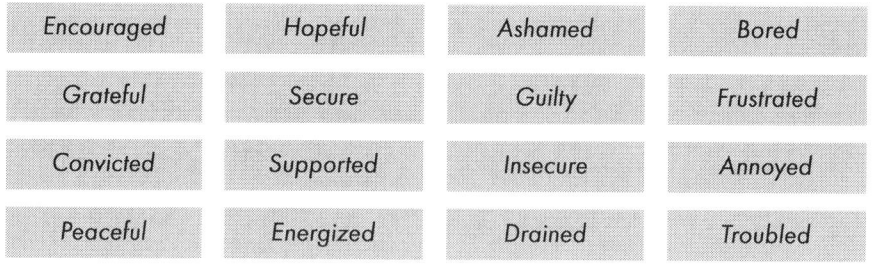

🖉 How would you describe your experience surveying your finances and your possessions? What thoughts and feelings arose in you as you considered what you have?

✎ Did you feel any desire to change what you saw, either by adding to it or subtracting from it? What do you think you would have gained if you had made the changes?

✎ How attached did you feel to your "earthly treasures"? If they were to be lost or taken away suddenly, how do you think you would react?

✎ How much time and energy do you think you give to tending to, growing and/or protecting your finances and your possessions?

✎ What do you suppose the current state of your finances and possessions says about the condition and focus of your heart?

Reflection

15-20 minutes

Find a quiet place to consider the questions below. Begin by reading the Scripture.

Do not lay up for yourselves treasures on earth, where moth and rust destroy and where thieves break in and steal, but lay up for yourselves treasures in heaven, where neither moth nor rust destroys and where thieves do not break in and steal. For where your treasure is, there your heart will be also.

No one can serve two masters, for either he will hate the one and love the other, or he will be devoted to the one and despise the other. You cannot serve God and money.

Matthew 6:19-21 & 24

✎ What thoughts and feelings do you experience as you read these words of Jesus?

✎ How do Jesus' words differ from "common, accepted religious wisdom" you've been taught regarding money and possessions?

- Do you believe that your heart has influence in your financial affairs or do you believe that you make choices regarding money and possessions purely with your mind? Why?

- Do you believe that the state of one's finances and possessions affects the condition of one's heart? What effect might your money be having on your heart?

- What do you think it looks like to serve money over God? Can you think of one example that you've seen in your life?

✏ What do you think it looks like to serve God over money? Can you think of one example that you've seen in your life?

✏ How have this week's exercises deepened your understanding of our Scripture passage?

GROUP DISCUSSION   30-60 MINUTES

Use the questions below to guide your group discussion. This week, we focused on Jesus' words in Matthew 6:19-21 & 24. Refer to the teachings and your experiences as you share together.

Read Matthew 6:19-21 & 24 aloud.

» What did you learn from the Scripture passage this week?

» What did you discover about yourself as you surveyed your "earthly treasures"?

» How do you think finances and possessions are affecting your relationship with God and others?

» How might your experiences this week affect your decisions regarding finances and possessions going forward?

» What would you like to ask God for as you consider going forward from here?

End the discussion with prayer.

Week 3
God Is A Giver

What then shall we say to these things? If God is for us, who can be against us? He who did not spare his own Son but gave him up for us all, how will he not also with him graciously give us all things?

Romans 8:31-32

The Lesson   15 minutes

Listen to the podcast for Week 3. It examines the hope and the challenges of moving our hearts' attachments from money to God. To help us do this, we consider how much we believe in God's generosity and love.

Real Life Practice   15-30 minutes

Answer the questions below to make an honest assessment of your current perspective and beliefs in God's generosity and love toward you. Find a quiet place where you won't be disturbed.

> As you answer the questions, you may be tempted to give "correct" or "Sunday School" type responses. Or, you may be tempted to be too harsh in your assessment of yourself. Try to resist these tendencies and answer the questions as honestly and straightforwardly as you can. Ask God for His help in doing this.

Read our focus verses for this week:

What then shall we say to these things? If God is for us, who can be against us? He who did not spare his own Son but gave him up for us all, how will he not also with him graciously give us all things?

Who shall separate us from the love of Christ? Shall tribulation, or distress, or persecution, or famine, or nakedness, or danger, or sword?

No, in all these things we are more than conquerors through him who loved us. For I am sure that neither death nor life, nor angels nor rulers, nor things present nor things to come, nor powers, nor height nor depth, nor anything else in all creation, will be able to separate us from the love of God in Christ Jesus our Lord.

Romans 8:31-32, 35, 37-39

✏ Think about your life and list a few specific things that God has provided for you.

✏ When you think about these provisions, would you say God has generally been withholding, adequate or generous to you?

✏ Think of a time in the recent past when you found yourself in need of something important to your life, such as money, work, housing, transportation, food, rest, health, companionship or care. What specific instance comes to mind? What were the circumstances that brought you to this situation of need?

- How do you remember reacting when you were in need? What did you think at the time? What did you feel? What actions did you take, if any?

- While you were in need, did you try to include God in your experience, either through prayer, Scripture, speaking with a pastor or fellow Christian(s) to gain God's perspective on the matter, etc.?

- As you look at your reactions and actions in this situation, what might they say about your everyday expectations and belief in God being a generous giver towards you?

- Now consider your belief in God's love for you. Given your life history, list a few specific times (if any) where you experienced God's love for you.

- What circumstances or situations tend to help you experience God's love?

- Do you ever feel separated from God's love? If so, what circumstances or situations tend to contribute to your feeling this way?

- How would you describe God in His relationship with you: absent, distant, impotent, merely present, fickle, gentle, friendly, warm, loving, strong, passionate?

✏ Look over your answers above. What might they say about your expectations and belief in God's love for you?

OBSERVATION NOTES   5-10 MINUTES

Spend a few minutes answering the following questions based on your experiences with the Real Life Practice.

Refer to the word chart below when answering.

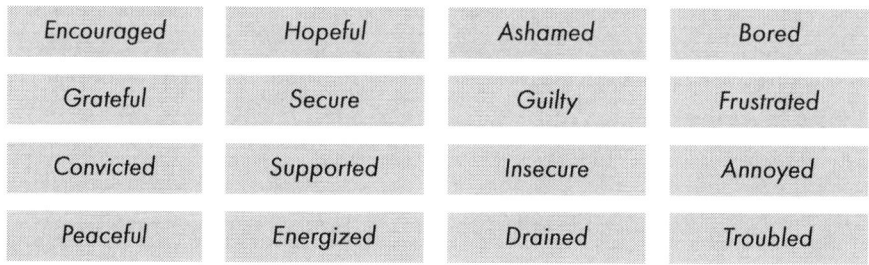

✏ How would you describe your experience in the Real Life Practice? What thoughts and feelings arose in you as you answered the questions?

- Were you tempted to be hard on yourself or paint yourself in a good light, either by adding to your answers or subtracting from them? What do you think you would have gained or avoided by giving into either temptation?

- Based on your answers from the Real Life Practice, how attached to God do you suppose that you are? What aspects of your life indicate that level of attachment to God?

- How much time and energy do you tend to give to cultivating, growing and/or nurturing a healthy relationship with God? What specifically do you do?

✏ What do you suppose might be different if you were able to fully live in the truth of God's generosity and love towards you?

REFLECTION   15-20 MINUTES

Find a quiet place to consider the questions below. Begin by reading the Scripture for this week.

> *What then shall we say to these things? If God is for us, who can be against us? He who did not spare his own Son but gave him up for us all, how will he not also with him graciously give us all things?*
>
> *Who shall separate us from the love of Christ? Shall tribulation, or distress, or persecution, or famine, or nakedness, or danger, or sword?*
>
> *No, in all these things we are more than conquerors through him who loved us. For I am sure that neither death nor life, nor angels nor rulers, nor things present nor things to come, nor powers, nor height nor depth, nor anything else in all creation, will be able to separate us from the love of God in Christ Jesus our Lord.*
>
> Romans 8:31-32, 35, 37-39

✏ What thoughts and feelings do you experience as you read these words of Jesus?

✏ What do you think a person gains by having one's heart attached to money or possessions?

✏ What do you think a person loses by being attached to money or possessions?

✏ By contrast, what do you think a person risks losing when they seek to become more attached to God?

✏ What do you think you could gain by becoming more attached to God?

✏ How have this week's exercises deepened your understanding of the Scripture passage?

Group Discussion 30-60 minutes

Use the questions below to guide your group discussion. This week, we considered what Paul wrote in Romans 8:31-32, 35, 37-39. Refer to the teachings and your experiences as you share together.

Read Romans 8:31-32, 35, 37-39 aloud.

» What did you learn from the Scripture passage?

» What did you discover **about yourself** as you looked at your expectations and beliefs in God's generosity and love?

» What did you discover **about God** as you looked at your expectations and beliefs in God's generosity and love?

» How might your experiences this week affect your decisions regarding your relationship with God in the future?

» What would you like to ask God for as you consider going forward from here?

End the discussion with prayer.

WEEK 4

Acknowledging Our History With Money

[Jesus] entered Jericho and was passing through. And behold, there was a man named Zacchaeus. He was a chief tax collector and was rich.

Luke 19:1-2

The Lesson 15 minutes

Listen to the podcast for Week 4. It considers how we have both a history and a reputation regarding our relationship with money. It also notes how Jesus wants to relate with us as we explore these aspects of our attachment to money.

Real Life Practice 20-30 minutes

Complete the two exercises below to examine your history and your reputation with money.

> *As you engage in the following exercises, remember that Jesus wants you to include Him as you complete them. It can help to imagine Jesus being present with you, relating to you much like He did with Zacchaeus. Acknowledge His presence and ask for His assistance to help you discover what He wants you to become aware of.*

Read our focus verses for this week:

> *[Jesus] entered Jericho and was passing through. And behold, there was a man named Zacchaeus. He was a chief tax collector and was rich. And he was seeking to see who Jesus was, but on account of the crowd he could not, because he was small in stature. So he ran on ahead and climbed up into a sycamore tree to see him, for he was about to pass that way. And when Jesus came to the place, he looked up and said to him, "Zacchaeus, hurry and come down, for I must stay at your house today." So he hurried and came down and received him joyfully. And when they saw it, they all grumbled, "He has gone in to be the guest of a man who is a sinner." And Zacchaeus stood and said to the Lord, "Behold, Lord, the half of my goods I give to the poor. And if I have defrauded anyone of anything, I restore it fourfold." And Jesus said to him, "Today salvation has come to this house, since he also is a son of Abraham. For the Son of Man came to seek and to save the lost."*
>
> *Luke 19:1-10*

Search me, O God, and know my heart!
Try me and know my thoughts!
And see if there be any grievous way in me,
and lead me in the way everlasting!

Psalm 139:23-24

1. Your History With Money

Ask Jesus to help you complete the following phrases with honesty. Write down the first answer that comes to mind.

- I've always thought money was…

- In my family, money created…

- My parents would talk about money as if…

- As a kid, I just assumed that when I grew up, money would…

- My dad thought money was…

- My mom's attitude toward money was…

- Rich people have always seemed…

- ✎ Poor people have always seemed…

- ✎ I was taught that God thinks money is…

- ✎ Money causes…

- ✎ At some point, I decided that money was…

- ✎ One mistake I made with money was…

- ✎ One wise choice I made with money was…

- ✎ Money provides…

- ✎ I believe money should be…

- ✎ If I trusted God more, then money would…

2. Your Reputation With Money

Ask Jesus to help you identify a friend that will give you honest feedback about your reputation with money. Contact your friend and ask them the following questions, noting their answers below:

✏ What would you say is my reputation with money? How do you think others would describe my relationship to money?

On each of the following 10 point scales, how would you rate the way you think people see my relationship with money?

Greedy — Generous
| 1 | 2 | 3 | 4 | 5 | 6 | 7 | 8 | 9 | 10 |

Obvious — Hidden
| 1 | 2 | 3 | 4 | 5 | 6 | 7 | 8 | 9 | 10 |

Obsessed — Lazy
| 1 | 2 | 3 | 4 | 5 | 6 | 7 | 8 | 9 | 10 |

Stressed — Relaxed
| 1 | 2 | 3 | 4 | 5 | 6 | 7 | 8 | 9 | 10 |

Yearning — Content
| 1 | 2 | 3 | 4 | 5 | 6 | 7 | 8 | 9 | 10 |

Squandering   Self-Controlled

| 1 | 2 | 3 | 4 | 5 | 6 | 7 | 8 | 9 | 10 |

Foolish   Shrewd

| 1 | 2 | 3 | 4 | 5 | 6 | 7 | 8 | 9 | 10 |

✏ Would you say that my attitudes towards money are similar to or different from most people in my environment (family, friends, co-workers, church, etc.)? What causes you come to this conclusion?

✏ Is there anything else about my reputation with money that you think would be helpful for me to know?

Thank your friend for their time and tell them that you value their feedback.

OBSERVATION NOTES   5-10 MINUTES

Spend a few minutes answering the following questions based on your experiences with the Real Life Practice.

Refer to the word chart below when answering.

Encouraged	Hopeful	Ashamed	Bored
Grateful	Secure	Guilty	Frustrated
Convicted	Supported	Insecure	Annoyed
Peaceful	Energized	Drained	Troubled

✎ How would you describe your experience examining your history with money in the first exercise? What thoughts and feelings arose in you as you completed the sentences?

✎ What general themes, attitudes or memories did you discover are a part of your history with money?

✎ How would you describe your experience talking with your friend about your reputation with money? What thoughts and feelings arose in you as you noted your friend's perspective?

✏ What themes and attitudes did you discover are a part of your reputation with money?

✏ Do you see any connections between your history with money and your current reputation with money?

✏ How do you suppose your history and reputation with money affects your current relationships with other people?

✏ How do you suppose your history and reputation with money affects your relationship with God?

Reflection   15-20 minutes

Find a quiet place to consider the questions below. Begin by reading the Scripture for this week.

> *[Jesus] entered Jericho and was passing through. And behold, there was a man named Zacchaeus. He was a chief tax collector and was rich. And he was seeking to see who Jesus was, but on account of the crowd he could not, because he was small in stature. So he ran on ahead and climbed up into a sycamore tree to see him, for he was about to pass that way. And when Jesus came to the place, he looked up and said to him, "Zacchaeus, hurry and come down, for I must stay at your house today." So he hurried and came down and received him joyfully. And when they saw it, they all grumbled, "He has gone in to be the guest of a man who is a sinner." And Zacchaeus stood and said to the Lord, "Behold, Lord, the half of my goods I give to the poor. And if I have defrauded anyone of anything, I restore it fourfold." And Jesus said to him, "Today salvation has come to this house, since he also is a son of Abraham. For the Son of Man came to seek and to save the lost."*
>
> *— Luke 19:1-10*

> *Search me, O God, and know my heart!*
>   *Try me and know my thoughts!*
> *And see if there be any grievous way in me,*
>   *and lead me in the way everlasting!*
>
> *— Psalm 139:23-24*

✎ What thoughts and feelings do you experience as you read the story of Zacchaeus and the verses from the Psalm?

✏ How did Zacchaeus' history and reputation with money affect his relationship with his community?

✏ How did Zacchaeus' history and reputation with money affect his relationship with Jesus?

✏ How did Jesus' relationship with Zacchaeus affect Zacchaeus' relationship to money?

✏ How do you think you would react if Jesus suddenly showed up and invited Himself into your home for the day? What would you be afraid of? What would you be hoping for?

✏ As you have opened your heart this week to God's searching, how would you sum up what He has revealed to you?

✏ How have this week's exercises deepened your understanding of the Scripture passages?

GROUP DISCUSSION 30-60 MINUTES

Use the questions below to guide your group discussion. This week, we considered the story of Jesus and Zacchaeus in Luke 19:1-10 and Psalm 139:23-24. Refer to the teachings and your experiences as you share together.

Read Luke 19:1-10 and Psalm 139:23-24 aloud.

» What did you learn from the Scripture passages?

» What did you discover about yourself as you looked at your history and reputation with money?

» What did you discover about how Jesus sees you and your history and reputation with money?

» How might your experiences this week affect your decisions regarding your relationship with money in the future?

» What would you like to ask God for as you consider going forward from here?

End the discussion with prayer.

Week 5

Our History With God And Money

And [Jesus] said, "There was a man who had two sons. And the younger of them said to his father, 'Father, give me the share of property that is coming to me.' And he divided his property between them. Not many days later, the younger son gathered all he had and took a journey into a far country, and there he squandered his property in reckless living."

Luke 15:11-13

The Lesson   15 minutes

Listen to the podcast for Week 5. It discusses how our relational history with God can be revealed by our attachments to money. By examining our actions and expectations around money, we can discover important assumptions we might have about God.

Real Life Practice   20-40 minutes

Answer the questions below to consider how your attachments to money relate to your relational history with God. Find a quiet place where you won't be disturbed. Ask God to lead you and guide you during this practice.

> *As you engage in the following exercise, remember God's character is the same, whether or not our assumptions about Him are accurate. If you discover you have been holding a wrong belief about God's character, remember that God will still continue to receive, love and accept you, just as the father in this parable receives, loves and accepts his sons.*

1. Like The Prodigal

Read the beginning of Jesus' parable, and then answer the questions below:

> *And [Jesus] said, "There was a man who had two sons. And the younger of them said to his father, 'Father, give me the share of property that is coming to me.' And he divided his property between them. Not many days later, the younger son gathered all he had and took a journey into a far country, and there he squandered his property in reckless living. And when he had spent everything, a severe famine arose in that country, and he began to be in need. So he went and hired himself out to one of the citizens of that country, who sent him into his fields to feed pigs. And he was longing to be fed with the pods that the pigs ate, and no one gave him anything."*
>
> *Luke 15:11-16*

✒ Have you ever taken an important financial action without including God in your decision-making process? What specific instance comes to mind? What were you trying to accomplish? How did that decision turn out?

✒ Did this financial action bring you closer in relationship to God or further away? How so?

✒ As you consider that decision and its ramifications, what might your actions reveal to you about how much you do or don't want God to be involved in your financial life? What difference do you think His presence might make?

✏ Think of a time when you squandered or were reckless with your resources. Ask God to bring a particular situation to your attention if you have a hard time thinking of one. What thoughts and feelings motivated your actions? Was your relationship with God a part of this experience? How do you feel about those actions now?

✏ Did this squandering of your resources bring you closer in relationship to God or further away? How so?

✏ As you consider that time in your life, what might that decision and its ramifications reveal about how you viewed the resources God entrusted to you?

2. Who Is This Father?

Read the middle part of Jesus' parable and answer the questions below:

> "But when [the prodigal son] came to himself, he said, 'How many of my father's hired servants have more than enough bread, but I perish here with hunger! I will arise and go to my father, and I will say to him, "Father, I have sinned against heaven and before you. I am no longer worthy to be called your son. Treat me as one of your hired servants."' And he arose and came to his father. But while he was still a long way off, his father saw him and felt compassion, and ran and embraced him and kissed him. And the son said to him, 'Father, I have sinned against heaven and before you. I am no longer worthy to be called your son.' But the father said to his servants, 'Bring quickly the best robe, and put it on him, and put a ring on his hand, and shoes on his feet. And bring the fattened calf and kill it, and let us eat and celebrate. For this my son was dead, and is alive again; he was lost, and is found.' And they began to celebrate."
>
> Luke 17:24

✏ How do you think God views your financial decisions, particularly the ones you made on your own, outside of your relationship with Him?

✏ Is there a part of your financial life right now where you are living and making decisions outside of your relationship with God? If so, what would it take for you to have a change of heart and action? What would it look like for you to come home to your Father?

3. Like the Older Brother

Read the last part of Jesus' parable and answer the questions below:

"Now his older son was in the field, and as he came and drew near to the house, he heard music and dancing. And he called one of the servants and asked what these things meant. And he said to him, 'Your brother has come, and your father has killed the fattened calf, because he has received him back safe and sound.' But he was angry and refused to go in. His father came out and entreated him, but he answered his father, 'Look, these many years I have served you, and I never disobeyed your command, yet you never gave me a young goat, that I might celebrate with my friends. But when this son of yours came, who has devoured your property with prostitutes, you killed the fattened calf for him!' And he said to him, 'Son, you are always with me, and all that is mine is yours. It was fitting to celebrate and be glad, for this your brother was dead, and is alive; he was lost, and is found.'"

Luke 15: 25-32

✏ Can you think of a time when you were critical or disapproving of how someone else handled their money or took care of their possessions? Ask God to bring a specific person to mind. What was the basis for your attitude?

✏ Did this situation bring you closer in relationship to God or further away? How so?

✏ What might your reaction to this situation say about your belief that you deserve or can earn God's provision and care?

- Have you ever felt jealous or envious of someone's undeserved good fortune? What were the circumstances? What seemed unfair to you about that situation?

- Did this situation bring you closer in relationship to God or further away? How so?

- What might your reaction to that situation tell you about your belief in God's character and generosity?

OBSERVATION NOTES 5-10 MINUTES

Spend a few minutes answering the following questions based on your experiences with the Real Life Practice.

Refer to the word chart below when answering.

Encouraged	Hopeful	Ashamed	Bored
Grateful	Secure	Guilty	Frustrated
Convicted	Supported	Insecure	Annoyed
Peaceful	Energized	Drained	Troubled

- What thoughts and feelings arose in you as you answered the questions that related to the younger son in the parable?

- In what ways did you relate with the younger son's attitudes toward the father?

- What thoughts and feelings arose in you as you answered the questions regarding the older son?

✏ In what ways did you relate with the older son's attitudes toward the father?

✏ What thoughts and feelings arose in you as you considered that the father in the story represents your Heavenly Father?

✏ What do you want to remember about God as you go forward?

Reflection   15-20 minutes

Find a quiet place to consider the questions below. Begin by reading the Scripture for this week.

> *And [Jesus] said, "There was a man who had two sons. And the younger of them said to his father, 'Father, give me the share of property that is coming to me.' And he divided his property*

between them. Not many days later, the younger son gathered all he had and took a journey into a far country, and there he squandered his property in reckless living. And when he had spent everything, a severe famine arose in that country, and he began to be in need. So he went and hired himself out to one of the citizens of that country, who sent him into his fields to feed pigs. And he was longing to be fed with the pods that the pigs ate, and no one gave him anything.

"But when he came to himself, he said, 'How many of my father's hired servants have more than enough bread, but I perish here with hunger! I will arise and go to my father, and I will say to him, "Father, I have sinned against heaven and before you. I am no longer worthy to be called your son. Treat me as one of your hired servants."' And he arose and came to his father. But while he was still a long way off, his father saw him and felt compassion, and ran and embraced him and kissed him. And the son said to him, 'Father, I have sinned against heaven and before you. I am no longer worthy to be called your son.' But the father said to his servants, 'Bring quickly the best robe, and put it on him, and put a ring on his hand, and shoes on his feet. And bring the fattened calf and kill it, and let us eat and celebrate. For this my son was dead, and is alive again; he was lost, and is found.' And they began to celebrate.

"Now his older son was in the field, and as he came and drew near to the house, he heard music and dancing. And he called one of the servants and asked what these things meant. And he said to him, 'Your brother has come, and your father has killed the fattened calf, because he has received him back safe and sound.' But he was angry and refused to go in. His father came out and entreated him, but he answered his father, 'Look, these many years I have served you, and I never disobeyed your command, yet you never gave me a young goat, that I might celebrate with my friends. But when this son of yours came, who has devoured your property with prostitutes, you killed the fattened calf for him!' And he said to him, 'Son, you are always with me, and all that is mine is yours. It was fitting to celebrate and be glad, for this your brother was dead, and is alive; he was lost, and is found.' "

Luke 15:11-23

✏ What thoughts and feelings do you experience as you consider again Jesus' parable of the prodigal son and his brother?

✏ In the parable, how does money reveal the false assumptions that the two sons held about their father?

✏ With which brother do you identify more—the prodigal son or the older brother? Why?

✎ In the parable, what does the father's attitude seem to be towards money?

✎ What does the father's attitude seem to be towards his sons?

✎ How have this week's exercises deepened your understanding of this parable and what it tells you about God?

GROUP DISCUSSION   30-60 MINUTES

Use the questions below to guide your group discussion. This week, we considered Jesus' parable of the prodigal son and his older brother in Luke 15:11-23. Refer to the teachings and your experiences as you share together.

Read Luke 15:11-23 aloud.

» What did you learn from the Scripture passages?

» What did you discover about yourself as you looked at how your attachments to money reveal your assumptions about God?

» What did you discover about how God sees you and your attachment to money?

» How might your experiences this week affect your decisions regarding your relationship with God in the future?

» What would you like to ask God for as you consider going forward from here?

End the discussion with prayer.

Week 6

What Is Our Current Identity?

And Jesus, looking at him, loved him, and said to him, "You lack one thing: go, sell all that you have and give to the poor, and you will have treasure in heaven; and come, follow me." Disheartened by the saying, he went away sorrowful, for he had great possessions.

Mark 10:21-22

The Lesson   15 minutes

Listen to the podcast for Week 6. It invites us to consider how our personal identity regarding money can affect our ability to follow God. An interaction with Jesus can be a powerful way to discover what attachments might be hindering us from our true identity as a follower of Jesus Christ.

Real Life Practice   15-30 minutes

Complete the exercises below to help discover your identity regarding money and possessions, and compare it with your true identity in Christ.

> *From our Scripture this week, it might be tempting to assume that Jesus wants us to simply sell all our possessions in order to better follow Him. The purpose of this exercise is to discover if money and possessions play a role in your identity and how this might hinder how you can follow Christ. Simply make note of what you discover. Let Jesus make the decisions about what actions you should take, if any.*

1. Discovering Your Financial Identity

Begin by reading our first Scripture for this week.

> *And as [Jesus] was setting out on his journey, a man ran up and knelt before him and asked him, "Good Teacher, what must I do to inherit eternal life?" And Jesus said to him, "Why do you call me good? No one is good except God alone. You know the commandments: 'Do not murder, Do not commit adultery, Do not steal, Do not bear false witness, Do not defraud, Honor your father and mother.'" And he said to him, "Teacher, all these I have kept from my youth." And Jesus, looking at him, loved him, and said to him, "You lack one thing: go, sell all that you have and give to the poor, and you will have treasure in*

heaven; and come, follow me." Disheartened by the saying, he went away sorrowful, for he had great possessions.
Mark 10:17-22

Choose an item from your possessions that is most treasured to you, something that is very special.

Complete the rest of this Real Life Practice with that item in your presence where you can see it and ponder it.

> The possession I will have in my presence during the rest of this exercise is
>
> ....

Answer the following questions. Refer to your treasured possession and to the lists you created in your Week 2 Real Life Practice as you do.

✎ Consider your current financial situation. What does the state of your finances communicate to you about the kind of person you are?

✎ What if your finances suddenly *increased* by 50% or more? What is your initial reaction to imagining that situation? What would you hope this financial increase would tell you about the kind of person you are? What do you fear it might communicate to you?

✏ What if circumstances suddenly *reduced* your finances by 50% or more? What is your initial reaction to imagining that situation? What would you hope this financial decrease would tell you about the kind of person you are? What do you fear it might communicate to you?

✏ Now, consider your possessions. What do your possessions communicate to you about the kind of person you are?

✏ What if you could suddenly *acquire* many more possessions? What would you add to what you already own? What is your initial reaction to imagining that situation? What would you hope having these additional possessions would tell you about the kind of person you are? What do you fear it might communicate to you?

✒ What if you suddenly *lost* 50% or more of your possessions? What is your initial reaction to imagining that situation? What would you hope losing so many possessions would tell you about the kind of person you are? What do you fear it might communicate to you?

✒ Now, consider the treasured possession that is before you. What does this specific possession communicate to you about the kind of person you are?

✒ What if God invited you to *give up* this possession? What is your initial reaction to imagining that situation? What would you hope your answer to that invitation would tell you about the kind of person you are? What do you fear it might communicate about you?

2. Your Identity With Jesus

Read our second passage this week:

For the word of God is living and active, sharper than any two-edged sword, piercing to the division of soul and of spirit, of joints and of marrow, and discerning the thoughts and intentions of the heart. And no creature is hidden from his sight, but all are naked and exposed to the eyes of him to whom we must give account.
Hebrews 4:12-13

Talk with Jesus about what you discovered about yourself and your attachment to your finances and possessions from the previous section.

Ask Him if your identity regarding your finances and possessions might be helping or hindering your ability to follow Him. Simply have a conversation with Jesus without expecting what Jesus' answers will be.

✎ Afterwards, write down what you both talked about.

Observation Notes

5-10 minutes

Spend a few minutes answering the following questions based on your experiences with the Real Life Practice.

Refer to the word chart below when answering.

Encouraged	Hopeful	Ashamed	Bored
Grateful	Secure	Guilty	Frustrated
Convicted	Supported	Insecure	Annoyed
Peaceful	Energized	Drained	Troubled

✏ How would you describe your experience examining your identity regarding finances and possessions? What thoughts and feelings arose in you as you answered the questions?

✏ What did you discover about your identity regarding finances and possessions?

✏ How would you describe your experience talking with Jesus about your identity regarding finances and possessions? What thoughts and feelings arose in you as you talked with Him?

✏ What did you discover about how Jesus sees you? How do you think He feels toward you?

✏ How much do you think your identity regarding money and possessions is helping or hindering your ability to follow Jesus?

Reflection   15-20 minutes

Find a quiet place to consider the questions below. Begin by reading the Scripture for this week.

> *And as [Jesus] was setting out on his journey, a man ran up and knelt before him and asked him, "Good Teacher, what must I do to inherit eternal life?" And Jesus said to him, "Why do you call me good? No one is good except God alone. You know the commandments: 'Do not murder, Do not commit adultery, Do not steal, Do not bear false witness, Do not defraud, Honor your father and mother.'" And he said to him, "Teacher, all these I have kept from my youth." And Jesus, looking at him, loved him, and said to him, "You lack one thing: go, sell all that you have and give to the poor, and you will have treasure in heaven; and come, follow me." Disheartened by the saying, he went away sorrowful, for he had great possessions.*
>
> *Mark 10:17-22*

For the word of God is living and active, sharper than any two-edged sword, piercing to the division of soul and of spirit, of joints and of marrow, and discerning the thoughts and intentions of the heart. And no creature is hidden from his sight, but all are naked and exposed to the eyes of him to whom we must give account.
Hebrew 4:12-13

🖉 What thoughts and feelings do you experience as you consider again the story of Jesus and the rich man?

🖉 What do you think Jesus revealed about the man when He asked Him to sell all of his possessions? Why do you think it was important for the man to know that about himself?

- How do you think Jesus felt about the man, even after the man went away sorrowful?

- What thoughts and feelings do you experience as you consider again the passage from Hebrews about how God's word affects us?

- How have this week's exercises deepened your understanding of these passages?

Group Discussion

30-60 minutes

Use the questions below to guide your group discussion. This week, we considered the story of Jesus and the rich man in Mark 10:17-22, as well as the passage in Hebrews 4:12-13. Refer to the teachings and your experiences as you share together.

Read Mark 10:17-22 and Hebrews 4:12-13 aloud.

- » What did you learn from the Scripture passages?

- » What did you discover about yourself as you looked at your identity regarding your finances and possessions?

- » What did you discover about how Jesus sees you and your identity regarding money and possessions?

- » How might your experiences this week affect your identity in the future?

- » What would you like to ask God for as you consider going forward from here?

End the discussion with prayer.

Week 7

Using Money To Create A Reputation

Now the full number of those who believed were of one heart and soul, and no one said that any of the things that belonged to him was his own, but they had everything in common.

But a man named Ananias, with his wife Sapphira, sold a piece of property, and with his wife's knowledge he kept back for himself some of the proceeds and brought only a part of it and laid it at the apostles' feet.

Acts 4:32 & 5:1

The Lesson 15 minutes

Listen to the podcast for Week 7. It considers how we could be using money to create a reputation for ourselves in the eyes of others. It discusses God's perspective on our desire to be seen by others and how our attachment to a reputation might be keeping us from financial and spiritual freedom.

Real Life Practice 15-30 minutes

Complete the exercises below to discover how you might be using money and possessions to create a reputation for yourself with others.

> As you examine what your actions might reveal about your heart, you could be tempted to either gloss over your sin or be overly judgmental and punishing of yourself. As you work through this exercise, try to avoid either extreme. None of us are sinless, nor are any of our choices so shameful that we are without hope. God is already aware of what is happening in your life and in your heart, and through Jesus Christ, He forgives you and accepts you with love. Invite God to lead you through this exercise, and stay close to Him as He reveals your heart to you.

1. Putting Forth A Reputation

Read the first part of the focus story for this week.

> *Now the full number of those who believed were of one heart and soul, and no one said that any of the things that belonged to him was his own, but they had everything in common.*
>
> *But a man named Ananias, with his wife Sapphira, sold a piece of property, and with his wife's knowledge he kept back for himself some of the proceeds and brought only a part of it and laid it at the apostles' feet.*
>
> *Acts 4:32 & 5:1*

Answer the following questions about what kind of financial reputation you tend to desire. Be as honest as you can with yourself and with God.

- In Week 4 of *No Strings,* you asked a friend for feedback about your financial reputation (page 45). As you reconsider that experience, did any of your friend's answers bother you? If so, what troubled you and why?

- How would you like other people to see you and your relationship with money and possessions? What would you like your financial reputation to be? With your friends? With your family? Within your church? Within society?

- What possessions do you display or what actions do you take in order to communicate to other people this financial reputation? Consider why you chose where you live, your mode of transportation, your clothing, schools attended by you or your children, people you spend time with, places you frequent, charities you support, etc.

✏ Are any of these things you display or actions you take a stretch for you to make happen? Have any of them started to feel like a burden to maintain?

✏ Look over your financial survey from Week 2 (page 20). Is there some aspect of your money or possessions—the amount, the way you're using them, what you're spending money on, the level of your debt—that you would feel uncomfortable or embarrassed if other people knew about?

✏ What is it about that aspect of your financial situation that you prefer to keep private or hidden?

✏ What are you afraid would happen if other people knew about what you're keeping hidden? What do you expect would change in their estimation of you?

2. Coming Clean

Read this excerpt from this week's passage from Acts:

But Peter said, "Ananias, why has Satan filled your heart to lie to the Holy Spirit and to keep back for yourself part of the proceeds of the land? While it remained unsold, did it not remain your own? And after it was sold, was it not at your disposal? Why is it that you have contrived this deed in your heart? You have not lied to man but to God."

Acts 5:3-4

Talk with the Lord about what you discovered from the previous section. Tell Him what you have learned about yourself and your desire to create a financial reputation in the eyes of others.

Confess to God how you have been using your finances and possessions in order to affect how people see you, by consciously presenting something and/or in keeping something secret. Speak back to God the truth that He already knows.

Receive God's love and forgiveness through Christ's atoning sacrifice on the cross, and ask God to help you live a more honest financial life with Him and others.

Ask God if there might be someone that He thinks you should also share this truth with. Pay attention to any names that come to mind and ask God to confirm what you should share with this person.

If you feel led to share the truth with this person, talk with them this week. If no one specific comes to mind, simply thank God for His attention, love and care for you.

Observation Notes

5-10 minutes

Spend a few minutes answering the following questions based on your experiences with the Real Life Practice.

Refer to the word chart below when answering.

Encouraged	Hopeful	Ashamed	Bored
Grateful	Secure	Guilty	Frustrated
Convicted	Supported	Insecure	Annoyed
Peaceful	Energized	Drained	Troubled

- How would you describe your experience examining your desires to create a financial reputation with others? What thoughts and feelings arose in you as you answered the questions?

- What habits did you discover you have in maintaining your financial reputation with others?

- How would you describe your experience confessing to God how you have been using your finances and possessions to affect how people see you? What thoughts and feelings arose in you as you talked with Him?

✏ If you were led to share with another person this week, how would you describe that experience? What thoughts and feelings did you have as you shared with this person?

✏ What did you discover about how your desire to have a financial reputation might be affecting your ability to love others?

Reflection   15-20 minutes

Find a quiet place to consider the questions below. Begin by reading the Scripture for this week.

> *Now the full number of those who believed were of one heart and soul, and no one said that any of the things that belonged to him was his own, but they had everything in common. And with great power the apostles were giving their testimony to the resurrection of the Lord Jesus, and great grace was upon them all. There was not a needy person among them, for as many as were owners of lands or houses sold them and brought the proceeds of what was sold and laid it at the apostles' feet, and it was distributed to each as any had need. Thus Joseph, who was also called by the apostles Barnabas (which means son of encouragement), a Levite, a native of Cyprus, sold a field that belonged to him and brought the money and laid it at the apostles' feet. Now the full number of those who believed were of one heart and soul, and no one said that any of the things*

that belonged to him was his own, but they had everything in common.

But a man named Ananias, with his wife Sapphira, sold a piece of property, and with his wife's knowledge he kept back for himself some of the proceeds and brought only a part of it and laid it at the apostles' feet. But Peter said, "Ananias, why has Satan filled your heart to lie to the Holy Spirit and to keep back for yourself part of the proceeds of the land? While it remained unsold, did it not remain your own? And after it was sold, was it not at your disposal? Why is it that you have contrived this deed in your heart? You have not lied to man but to God." When Ananias heard these words, he fell down and breathed his last. And great fear came upon all who heard of it. The young men rose and wrapped him up and carried him out and buried him.

After an interval of about three hours his wife came in, not knowing what had happened. And Peter said to her, "Tell me whether you sold the land for so much." And she said, "Yes, for so much." But Peter said to her, "How is it that you have agreed together to test the Spirit of the Lord? Behold, the feet of those who have buried your husband are at the door, and they will carry you out." Immediately she fell down at his feet and breathed her last. When the young men came in they found her dead, and they carried her out and buried her beside her husband. And great fear came upon the whole church and upon all who heard of these things.

Acts 4:32-37 & 5:1-11

✎ What thoughts and feelings do you have as you read about the financial transparency and freedom of the early Christian church? What do you think it would be like to be a part of that community?

- What thoughts and feelings do you experience as you consider again what happened with Ananias and Sapphira?

- From your perspective, do you think that the consequences of Ananias and Sapphira's actions fit the seriousness of their sin? Why or why not?

- If God had not made an example of Ananias and Sapphira, what impact do you suppose their actions might have had on the rest of their Christian community? Why?

✏ What impact might your heart issues regarding a financial reputation have on the people around you?

✏ How have this week's exercises deepened your understanding of the Scripture passage?

Group Discussion   30-60 minutes

Use the questions below to guide your group discussion. This week, we considered the story of Ananias and Sapphira from the early Christian church in Acts 4:32-37 & 5:1-11. Refer to the teachings and your experiences as you share together.

Read Acts 4:32-37 & 5:1-11 aloud.

- » What did you learn from the Scripture passages?

- » What did you discover about yourself as you looked at your heart tendencies to create a financial reputation in the eyes of others?

- » What did you discover about how God feels about us using money to create a false financial reputation?

- » How might your experiences this week affect how you relate to others regarding money in the future?

- » What would you like to ask God for as you consider going forward from here?

End the discussion with prayer.

Week 8

In God We Trust

"But if God so clothes the grass of the field, which today is alive and tomorrow is thrown into the oven, will he not much more clothe you, O you of little faith? Therefore do not be anxious, saying, 'What shall we eat?' or 'What shall we drink?' or 'What shall we wear?' For the Gentiles seek after all these things, and your heavenly Father knows that you need them all."

Matthew 6:30-32

The Lesson 15 minutes

Listen to the podcast for Week 8. It examines how we could be more attached to money for our day-to-day security than being reliant on God to provide for our needs. We are reminded that whether we are in wealth or poverty, we could be forgetting that God highly values us and our needs and that He is more trustworthy than money.

Real Life Practice 15-20 minutes

Spend time in nature during the exercise below in order to better understand what or who you depend on to meet your needs.

> *Take time to ponder what you see during this exercise. Give yourself time to take it in before writing down your answers. Jesus is the one who invited us to consider what God is telling us through nature. Ask Jesus to reveal to you what He wants to communicate to you through nature in this exercise.*

Consider The Birds And Flowers

Go to a location where you can view nature. It could be a garden, a park, a field, a nature reserve, or anywhere where you can see both birds and flowers. If the weather is disagreeable to being outside, find a window that looks out onto nature. If blooms aren't in season, consider purchasing some flowers. Set them by the window so that you can observe them as well as what is outside.

Find a comfortable spot where you can freely observe and ask God to guide your observations and thoughts during this exercise.

Begin by spending about 5 minutes quietly observing the nature that you see around you. Take time to pay attention to what you see and hear.

Then, read this week's Scripture passage:

> "Therefore I tell you, do not be anxious about your life, what you will eat or what you will drink, nor about your body, what you will put on. Is not life more than food, and the body more than clothing? Look at the birds of the air: they neither sow nor

reap nor gather into barns, and yet your heavenly Father feeds them. Are you not of more value than they? And which of you by being anxious can add a single hour to his span of life? And why are you anxious about clothing? Consider the lilies of the field, how they grow: they neither toil nor spin, yet I tell you, even Solomon in all his glory was not arrayed like one of these. But if God so clothes the grass of the field, which today is alive and tomorrow is thrown into the oven, will he not much more clothe you, O you of little faith? Therefore do not be anxious, saying, 'What shall we eat?' or 'What shall we drink?' or 'What shall we wear?' For the Gentiles seek after all these things, and your heavenly Father knows that you need them all. But seek first the kingdom of God and his righteousness, and all these things will be added to you."

Matthew 6:24-33

✏ What do you tend to feel anxious about?

✏ How do you usually try to calm your anxiety about these things?

✏ Do you ever turn to money—either your possession of it, your ability to spend it or your desire to possess or spend it—as a solution to your anxieties? If so, how? What do you do?

✏ When does money tend to calm your anxieties? When does money tend to increase your anxieties?

✏ As you observe nature, what do the birds and flowers appear to be anxious about?

✏ How does God appear to express His love for the birds and the flowers?

✏️ How might God want to similarly express His love to you?

✏️ If God invited you to trust Him the way birds and flowers do, what would that specifically mean to you and the way you live your life?

✏️ How would you like to express your trust in God's love and thank Him for His care for you today? Share with God your answer to this question.

Observation Notes

5-10 minutes

Spend a few minutes answering the following questions based on your experiences with the Real Life Practice.

Refer to the word chart below when answering.

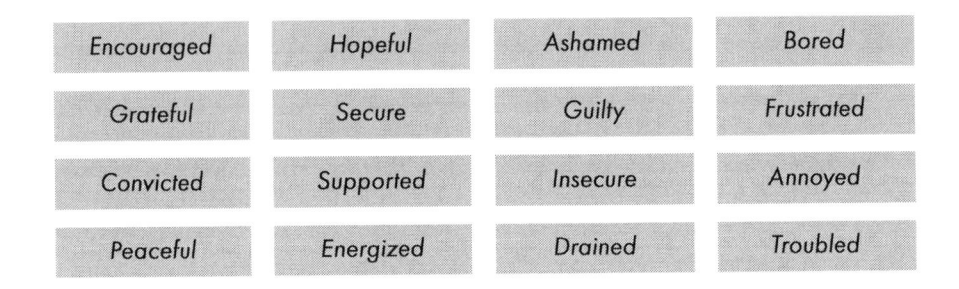

Encouraged	Hopeful	Ashamed	Bored
Grateful	Secure	Guilty	Frustrated
Convicted	Supported	Insecure	Annoyed
Peaceful	Energized	Drained	Troubled

- How would you describe your experience considering your anxieties and how you tend to calm them? What thoughts and feelings arose in you as you answered the questions?

- Where did you discover that you usually look for your security?

- How would you describe your experience observing the birds and the flowers? What thoughts and feelings arose in you as you considered how God expresses His love to and through them?

✏︎ What did you discover about how your attachment to money might be affecting your ability to trust in God?

Reflection   15-20 minutes

Find a quiet place to consider the questions below. Begin by reading the Scripture for this week.

> *"Therefore I tell you, do not be anxious about your life, what you will eat or what you will drink, nor about your body, what you will put on. Is not life more than food, and the body more than clothing? Look at the birds of the air: they neither sow nor reap nor gather into barns, and yet your heavenly Father feeds them. Are you not of more value than they? And which of you by being anxious can add a single hour to his span of life? And why are you anxious about clothing? Consider the lilies of the field, how they grow: they neither toil nor spin, yet I tell you, even Solomon in all his glory was not arrayed like one of these. But if God so clothes the grass of the field, which today is alive and tomorrow is thrown into the oven, will he not much more clothe you, O you of little faith? Therefore do not be anxious, saying, 'What shall we eat?' or 'What shall we drink?' or 'What shall we wear?' For the Gentiles seek after all these things, and your heavenly Father knows that you need them all. But seek first the kingdom of God and his righteousness, and all these things will be added to you."*
>
> *Matthew 6:24-33*

✏ What thoughts and feelings do you have as you read Jesus' commandments about the cares and worries of this life?

✏ If someone were to depend on money to provide for all their needs, how could that attachment affect their relationship with God?

✏ What do you think Jesus means when He encourages us to "seek first the kingdom of God and his righteousness" instead of being "anxious about your life?"

Now read the second Scripture for this week:

> *Rejoice in the Lord always; again I will say, rejoice. Let your reasonableness be known to everyone. The Lord is at hand; do not be anxious about anything, but in everything by prayer and supplication with thanksgiving let your requests be made known to God. And the peace of God, which surpasses all understanding, will guard your hearts and your minds in Christ Jesus.*
>
> Philippians 4:4-7

✏ How might prayer and thanksgiving help untangle someone's heart strings that are attached to money for security?

✏ How might prayer and thanksgiving help you trust more in God for your sense of security?

✏ How have this week's exercises deepened your understanding of these passages?

Group Discussion

30-60 minutes

Use the questions below to guide your group discussion. This week, we considered Jesus' words in Matthew 6:24-33 and Paul's words in Philippians 4:4-7. Refer to the teachings and your experiences as you share together.

Read Matthew 6:23-44 and Philippians 4:4-7 aloud.

- » What did you learn from the Scripture passages?

- » What did you discover about yourself as you considered how you might use money for your sense of security?

- » What did you discover about how God wants us to trust in Him for our security?

- » How might your experiences this week affect how you react in the future when you become anxious about your needs?

- » What would you like to ask God for as you consider going forward from here?

End the discussion with prayer.

Week 9

Trusting God Together

And all who believed were together and had all things in common. And they were selling their possessions and belongings and distributing the proceeds to all, as any had need.
Acts 2:44-45

The Lesson   15 minutes

Listen to the podcast for Week 9. It discusses how the early church was led to meet one another's needs. It also considers how the Holy Spirit might be inviting us to be a part of God's provision to one another in our Christian communities today.

Real Life Practice   15-20 minutes

Answer the questions below to discern how the Holy Spirit might be inviting you to participate more in the flow of provisions within your church community.

> *This week's practice focuses on your relationship with a Christian community. If you are not currently a part of a Christian community, such as a local church or smaller group of Christians, talk with God about whether joining or increasing your participation in a local body of believers is the Real Life Practice you should engage in this week instead.*

Read the Scripture passage:

And they devoted themselves to the apostles' teaching and the fellowship, to the breaking of bread and the prayers. And awe came upon every soul, and many wonders and signs were being done through the apostles. And all who believed were together and had all things in common. And they were selling their possessions and belongings and distributing the proceeds to all, as any had need. And day by day, attending the temple together and breaking bread in their homes, they received their food with glad and generous hearts, praising God and having favor with all the people. And the Lord added to their number day by day those who were being saved.
Acts 2:42-47

1. Consider The Outflow

Pray about the Christian community that you are a part of. Focus your prayer on your local church body or a smaller community/activity/study group that you are a part of and/or serve.

- As you consider this Christian community with God, ask Him to remind you of or reveal to you any particular needs one or more members of the group might be experiencing right now. The needs could be financial, practical, emotional, or spiritual in nature. Write down whatever comes to mind.

- Next, ask God if He would like you to contribute to helping meet one or more of these needs. Pay attention to what comes to your mind. Write down what actions (if any) you sense God might be inviting you to take.

✏ How do you feel about these possible actions for members of your community? Pay attention to how you react internally to the thought of executing these ideas. If you feel excited, talk with God about your expectations. If you feel nervous or resistant, talk with God about your hesitations. Write down your thoughts and feelings below.

✏ What positive or negative things might come from you helping to meet this need? How might your actions possibly affect the other person? Yourself? The group? God and His desires?

✏ If you and God come to a conclusion together about an action to help meet the needs of someone in your Christian community, write out the next steps you could take this week to do so.

2. Consider The Inflow

- Do you personally have a need you are experiencing in your life? Consider areas that are financial, practical, emotional, or spiritual in nature. Talk with God and ask Him to reveal to you if there is an aspect of your life that could be helped by someone else's assistance. Write down what you discover.

- Talk with God about whether you should share this need with your Christian community or not. What do you think and feel about expressing your need to this group? How do you think they would respond? What would be your hopes? What would be your fears? Write down whatever you discover.

- What positive or negative things might come from you allowing your need to be met by the group? How might their actions possibly affect you? The person(s) who meet your need? The group? God and His desires?

✏ If you and God come to a conclusion together about sharing a personal need with your Christian community, write down whatever next steps you think you could take this week.

Observation Notes 5-10 minutes

Spend a few minutes answering the following questions based on your experiences with the Real Life Practice.

Refer to the word chart below when answering.

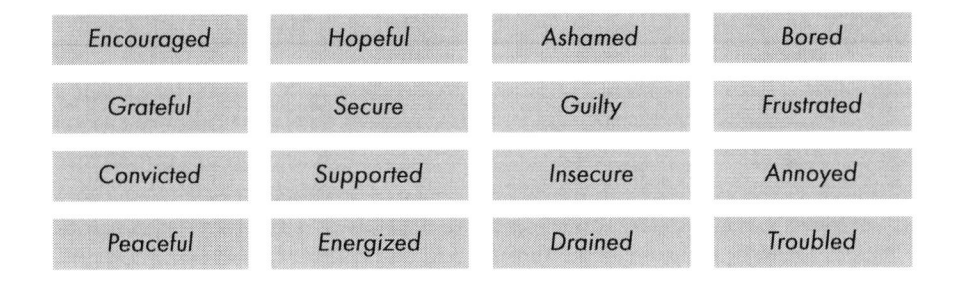

Encouraged	Hopeful	Ashamed	Bored
Grateful	Secure	Guilty	Frustrated
Convicted	Supported	Insecure	Annoyed
Peaceful	Energized	Drained	Troubled

✏ How would you describe your experience considering how you could help meet the needs of others in your Christian community? What thoughts and feelings arose in you as you prayed and answered the questions?

🖉 What attitudes did you discover you hold regarding your ability to be a part of God's provision to others in His church?

🖉 How would you describe your experience considering whether to invite your Christian community to help meet your personal need? What thoughts and feelings arose in you as you prayed and answered the questions?

🖉 What attitudes did you discover you hold regarding your ability to receive God's provision through others in His church?

🖉 What did you discover about how your attachment to money and possessions for security might be affecting your ability to participate in God's flow of provision within the Body of Christ?

Reflection 15-20 minutes

Find a quiet place to consider the questions below. Begin by reading the Scripture for this week.

> *And they devoted themselves to the apostles' teaching and the fellowship, to the breaking of bread and the prayers. And awe came upon every soul, and many wonders and signs were being done through the apostles. And all who believed were together and had all things in common. And they were selling their possessions and belongings and distributing the proceeds to all, as any had need. And day by day, attending the temple together and breaking bread in their homes, they received their food with glad and generous hearts, praising God and having favor with all the people. And the Lord added to their number day by day those who were being saved.*
>
> Acts 2:42-47

✎ What thoughts and feelings do you have as you read this description of how God led the early church members to care for one another?

✎ How do you think these actions of the early church affected everyone's relationships with each other within the local Body?

✏ How do you think the actions of the early church affected the members' understanding of God and His care for them?

✏ If a church body exhibited this kind of generosity and care for one another today, how do you think that would impact the church members in their day-to-day life?

✏ If a church body were to exhibit this level of generosity and care for one another today, how do you think this would impact people outside the church?

✏ How have this week's exercises deepened your understanding of this passage?

Group Discussion

30-60 MINUTES

Use the questions below to guide your group discussion. This week, we considered the description of the early church in Acts 2:42-47. Refer to the teachings and your experiences as you share together.

Read Acts 2:42-47 aloud.

- » What did you learn from the Scripture passage?

- » What did you discover about yourself as you considered how God might want to meet your needs and the needs of others within your Christian community?

- » What did you discover about how God might want to use the church in His provision for all its members?

- » How might your experiences this week affect how you interact with your church community regarding needs and provision in the future?

- » What would you like to ask God for as you consider going forward from here?

End the discussion with prayer.

Week 10

Contentment: A Sign Of Freedom

Not that I am speaking of being in need, for I have learned in whatever situation I am to be content. I know how to be brought low, and I know how to abound. In any and every circumstance, I have learned the secret of facing plenty and hunger, abundance and need. I can do all things through him who strengthens me.

Philippians 4:11-13

The Lesson · 15 minutes

Listen to the podcast for Week 10. It looks at Paul's example and teaching about financial contentment. It considers how deepening one's relational attachment to Jesus Christ can lead us toward freedom in all financial circumstances.

Real Life Practice · 15-30 minutes

Answer the questions below to practice increased contentment through stronger attachment to and dependence on Jesus Christ.

> *This week, you will be exploring a way to relate to Jesus that can help Him bring about lasting change in your heart. If you struggle to know and understand what's happening in your heart, pay attention to your desires, actions and emotions. These can help reveal to you where your heart might be attached to something other than to Jesus.*

Read the Scripture passage:

I rejoiced in the Lord greatly that now at length you have revived your concern for me. You were indeed concerned for me, but you had no opportunity. Not that I am speaking of being in need, for I have learned in whatever situation I am to be content. I know how to be brought low, and I know how to abound. In any and every circumstance, I have learned the secret of facing plenty and hunger, abundance and need. I can do all things through him who strengthens me.

Yet it was kind of you to share my trouble. And you Philippians yourselves know that in the beginning of the gospel, when I left Macedonia, no church entered into partnership with me in giving and receiving, except you only. Even in Thessalonica you sent me help for my needs once and again. Not that I seek the gift, but I seek the fruit that increases to your credit. I have received full payment, and more. I am well supplied, having received from Epaphroditus the gifts you sent, a fragrant offering, a sacrifice acceptable and pleasing to God. And my

God will supply every need of yours according to his riches in glory in Christ Jesus. To our God and Father be glory forever and ever. Amen.

Philippians 4:10-20

1. Assess Your Attachments

- How would you describe your financial situation right now? Are you brought low or abounding, in plenty or in hunger, in abundance or in need?

- How attached would you say you are right now to money and possessions? Note that you could be attached to what you have, to the desire to gain more, or to living as frugally as possible. If you are not sure how to answer this, consider how you would react should you lose what you have, never get the more that you want or be given the responsibility of more things than you need.

- In all honesty, how attached would you say that you are right now to Jesus Christ? How deeply do you think you trust Him to meet all your needs?

2. Growing In Trust And Contentment

- Ask God to help you identify a particular financial attachment you have right now. It could be an attachment to something that you possess or something that you are worried about not possessing. Again, consider what would cause you distress if you lost it or couldn't gain it. Write down what comes to mind.

- Share with Jesus any thoughts you've had, actions you've taken, and/or emotional reactions you've had regarding this financial attachment. Note below what you tell Him.

✏ What do you really want? Tell Jesus what your desires are regarding this financial attachment. Be as honest as you can with Him, even if what you want seems silly, petty or insecure. Tell Jesus what you would like to have happen in this situation. Write below what you tell Him.

✏ If Jesus were to allow to happen what you have just told Him, how do you think that would affect your relationship with Him? How would you react toward Him?

✏ Now suppose if Jesus were to allow to happen the opposite of what you want in this situation. What is your reaction to that thought?

✏ If Jesus were to allow the opposite of what you'd like to have happen, how do you think that would affect your relationship with Him? How do you think you would react toward Him?

✏ What if whatever Jesus allowed to happen in this situation came out of His love for you? Would that truth help you be willing to let go of your desires and this attachment and allow Jesus to handle it however He pleases?

If you are ready, confess to Jesus what you have discovered about your heart's attachment to this financial situation. Tell Him that—as much as you are able—you are releasing your desires and your will regarding the outcome of this circumstance. Tell Christ that, instead, you are welcoming His will to be done, whatever He chooses that to be.

End your time by asking Jesus to help you grow more in contentment through your relationship with Him.

Observation Notes

5-10 minutes

Spend a few minutes answering the following questions based on your experiences with the Real Life Practice.

Refer to the word chart below when answering.

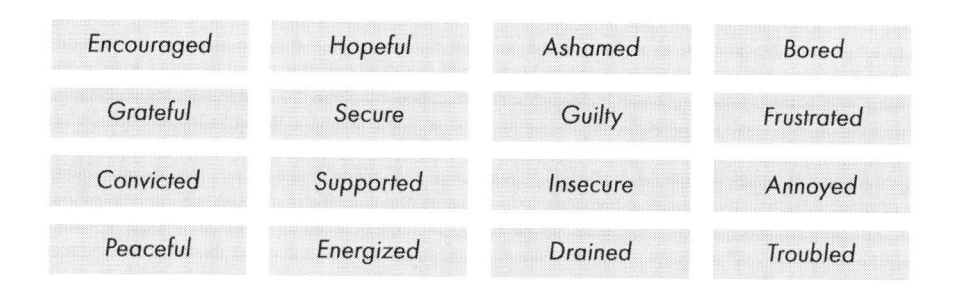

Encouraged	Hopeful	Ashamed	Bored
Grateful	Secure	Guilty	Frustrated
Convicted	Supported	Insecure	Annoyed
Peaceful	Energized	Drained	Troubled

- How would you describe your experience assessing your current attachments to finances and to Jesus? What thoughts and feelings arose in you as you answered the questions?

- In what type of financial circumstances do you find you struggle most with contentment: in plenty or in want?

- What habits do you exhibit when you feel yourself discontent?

✏ How would you describe your experience talking to Jesus about releasing your particular financial attachment? What thoughts and feelings arose in you as you prayed?

✏ What did you feel as you put your trust in Jesus regarding this particular financial situation?

✏ What did you discover about how deeper attachment to Jesus Christ can lead to experiencing contentment?

Reflection

15-20 minutes

Find a quiet place to answer the questions below. Begin by reading the Scripture passage for this week.

> *I rejoiced in the Lord greatly that now at length you have revived your concern for me. You were indeed concerned for me, but you had no opportunity. Not that I am speaking of being in need, for I have learned in whatever situation I am to be content. I know how to be brought low, and I know how to abound. In any and every circumstance, I have learned the secret of facing plenty and hunger, abundance and need. I can do all things through him who strengthens me.*
>
> *Yet it was kind of you to share my trouble. And you Philippians yourselves know that in the beginning of the gospel, when I left Macedonia, no church entered into partnership with me in giving and receiving, except you only. Even in Thessalonica you sent me help for my needs once and again. Not that I seek the gift, but I seek the fruit that increases to your credit. I have received full payment, and more. I am well supplied, having received from Epaphroditus the gifts you sent, a fragrant offering, a sacrifice acceptable and pleasing to God. And my God will supply every need of yours according to his riches in glory in Christ Jesus. To our God and Father be glory forever and ever. Amen.*
>
> *Philippians 4:10-20*

- What thoughts and feelings do you have as you read Paul's response to the Philippian church regarding their financial gift?

✏ How do you think a strong relational attachment to Christ could result in someone experiencing contentment in all variation of financial circumstances?

✏ What effect do you think contentment might have on your attachments to money and possessions?

✏ How do you think you could learn to grow in contentment over time?

✏ What effect do you think contentment might have on someone's willingness to share their money and possessions with others?

✏ How have this week's exercises deepened your understanding of this passage?

Group Discussion
30-60 MINUTES

Use the questions below to guide your group discussion. This week, we pondered Paul's writings in Philippians 4:10-20. Refer to the teachings and your experiences as you share together.

Read Philippians 4:10-20 aloud.

- » What did you learn from the Scripture passage?

- » What did you discover about yourself as you practiced deepening your attachment to Jesus?

- » What did you learn about how attachment to Christ can result in increased contentment regarding finances?

- » How might your experiences this week affect how you interact with Jesus in the future, particularly regarding your money and possessions?

- » What would you like to ask God for as you consider going forward from here?

End the discussion with prayer.

WEEK 11

Free To Choose

For I can testify that they gave not only what they could afford, but far more. And they did it of their own free will. They begged us again and again for the privilege of sharing in the gift for the believers in Jerusalem. They even did more than we had hoped, for their first action was to give themselves to the Lord and to us, just as God wanted them to do.
2 Corinthians 8:3-5 (NLT)

The Lesson 15 minutes

Listen to the podcast for Week 11. It looks at Paul's encouragement to the Corinthian church to give freely and generously to their fellow brothers and sisters in Christ. It considers that our financial freedom allows us to choose how to care for others out of loving and joyous hearts.

Real Life Practice 20-40 minutes

Follow the instructions below to examine your habit of giving and how God might be inviting you to grow in freedom in this area.

> As you look at your tendencies toward giving, you might experience feelings of guilt, shame, or pride. Instead of trying to cover those feelings up or ignore them, talk with God about them. Share with God your concerns and receive His forgiveness. Remember, God is fully aware of your heart, and His love for you is unceasing.

Read the beginning of this week's Scripture passage:

Now I want you to know, dear brothers and sisters, what God in his kindness has done through the churches in Macedonia. They are being tested by many troubles, and they are very poor. But they are also filled with abundant joy, which has overflowed in rich generosity.

For I can testify that they gave not only what they could afford, but far more. And they did it of their own free will. They begged us again and again for the privilege of sharing in the gift for the believers in Jerusalem. They even did more than we had hoped, for their first action was to give themselves to the Lord and to us, just as God wanted them to do.
2 Corinthians 8:1-5 (NLT)

1. Assess Your Giving

- Examine your general giving habits. Look over your financial records and note what Christian kingdom work you contribute to financially. (This is just for your awareness. You won't have to share this information with anyone.) Consider what you give to your church, to other Christian organizations and to Christian individuals. How do you feel about your current level of giving: is it too much, not enough or just right?

- How do you tend to make decisions about what to give and to whom you give?

- What tends to motivate you to give? Some of us give impulsively, perhaps even foolishly, when presented with needs. Others of us may be more frugal, maybe even miserly. Still others give mainly out of a sense of duty, obligation or expectation, while still others give in order to impress. Finally, some give wisely and freely out of joyful eagerness to be a part of God's work. What are your tendencies? Consider your history of giving and ask God to help you remember why you gave.

- ✏ What do you think your current giving communicates about your love for God's kingdom and the Body of Christ?

- ✏ Would you say that giving is a priority in your spiritual life? Why or why not?

- ✏ Now talk with God about your giving habits. Ask God if He desires you to continue what you're doing or to make some changes. Write down what comes to mind.

2. A Practice In Equality

Read the second half of this week's Scripture passage:

So we have urged Titus, who encouraged your giving in the first place, to return to you and encourage you to finish this ministry of giving. Since you excel in so many ways—in your faith, your gifted speakers, your knowledge, your enthusiasm, and your love from us—I want you to excel also in this gracious act of giving.

I am not commanding you to do this. But I am testing how genuine your love is by comparing it with the eagerness of the other churches.

You know the generous grace of our Lord Jesus Christ. Though he was rich, yet for your sakes he became poor, so that by his poverty he could make you rich.

Here is my advice: It would be good for you to finish what you started a year ago. Last year you were the first who wanted to give, and you were the first to begin doing it. Now you should finish what you started. Let the eagerness you showed in the beginning be matched now by your giving. Give in proportion to what you have. Whatever you give is acceptable if you give it eagerly. And give according to what you have, not what you don't have. Of course, I don't mean your giving should make life easy for others and hard for yourselves. I only mean that there should be some equality. Right now you have plenty and can help those who are in need. Later, they will have plenty and can share with you when you need it. In this way, things will be equal. As the Scriptures say,

"*Those who gathered a lot had nothing left over,
and those who gathered only a little had enough.*"
2 Corinthians 8:6-15 (NLT)

- Ask God to bring to mind a specific financial need in His kingdom. It could be for a family, a ministry, a church or a Christian organization doing God's work in your community or around the world. Write down what comes to mind.

- How much love do you feel for the people doing this particular kingdom work and the people they are serving? If you'd like to grow in your love, do some research on the work and the people involved. As you read stories, watch videos and/or talk to someone about this work, ask God to grow your love towards the people involved.

Next, ask God if He might be inviting you to demonstrate your love through contributing financially to this need.

If you sense God affirming that you should give, remember Paul's words as you continue to talk with God about how much to give:

> *Give in proportion to what you have. Whatever you give is acceptable if you give it eagerly. And give according to what you have, not what you don't have. (NLT)*

Then, give your financial gift. As you give it, thank God for the opportunity to participate in His kingdom work, and ask that this practice would grow and strengthen your heart for your brothers and sisters in Christ's Body and for the growth of God's kingdom.

OBSERVATION NOTES

5-10 MINUTES

Spend a few minutes answering the following questions based on your experiences with the Real Life Practice.

Refer to the word chart below when answering.

Encouraged	Hopeful	Ashamed	Bored
Grateful	Secure	Guilty	Frustrated
Convicted	Supported	Insecure	Annoyed
Peaceful	Energized	Drained	Troubled

✎ How would you describe your experience assessing your current giving habits? What thoughts and feelings arose in you as you answered the questions?

✎ What general themes or attitudes did you discover you hold regarding financial giving?

✏ How would you describe your experience as you gave to some specific kingdom work? What thoughts and feelings arose in you as you decided what and where to give financially?

✏ How did this practice of financial giving affect your spiritual life?

✏ What did you discover about how to choose wisely in the financial freedom that God has given you?

REFLECTION

15-20 MINUTES

Find a quiet place to answer the questions below. Begin by reading the Scripture passage for this week.

Now I want you to know, dear brothers and sisters, what God in his kindness has done through the churches in Macedonia. They are being tested by many troubles, and they are very poor. But they are also filled with abundant joy, which has overflowed in rich generosity.

For I can testify that they gave not only what they could afford, but far more. And they did it of their own free will. They begged us again and again for the privilege of sharing in the gift for the believers in Jerusalem. They even did more than we had hoped, for their first action was to give themselves to the Lord and to us, just as God wanted them to do.

So we have urged Titus, who encouraged your giving in the first place, to return to you and encourage you to finish this ministry of giving. Since you excel in so many ways—in your faith, your gifted speakers, your knowledge, your enthusiasm, and your love from us—I want you to excel also in this gracious act of giving.

I am not commanding you to do this. But I am testing how genuine your love is by comparing it with the eagerness of the other churches.

You know the generous grace of our Lord Jesus Christ. Though he was rich, yet for your sakes he became poor, so that by his poverty he could make you rich.

Here is my advice: It would be good for you to finish what you started a year ago. Last year you were the first who wanted to give, and you were the first to begin doing it. Now you should finish what you started. Let the eagerness you showed in the beginning be matched now by your giving. Give in proportion to what you have. Whatever you give is acceptable if you give it eagerly. And give according to what you have, not what you don't have. Of course, I don't mean your giving should make life easy for others and hard for yourselves. I only mean that there should be some equality. Right now you have plenty and can help those who are in need. Later, they will have plenty and can share with you when you need it. In this way, things will be equal. As the Scriptures say,

"*Those who gathered a lot had nothing left over,
and those who gathered only a little had enough.*"
2 Corinthians 8:1-15 (NLT)

✎ What thoughts and feelings do you have as you read Paul's encouragement to the Corinthian church regarding their financial giving?

✎ How might choosing to be dependent in our relationship with God affect our financial choices?

✎ If you made financial giving a spiritual priority, what difference do you think that would make in your life?

- How might growing in love affect your financial giving? Conversely, how might financial giving affect your growth in love?

- If Christians were to aim for financial equality in God's kingdom, what effect do you think that would have on our witness to the world?

- How have this week's exercises deepened your understanding of this passage?

GROUP DISCUSSION   30-60 MINUTES

Use the questions below to guide your group discussion. This week, we pondered Paul's teaching in 2 Corinthians 8:1-15. Refer to the teachings and your experiences as you share together.

Read 2 Corinthians 8:1-15 aloud.

- » What did you learn from the Scripture passage?

- » What did you discover about yourself as you assessed your giving habits and practiced giving a gift with God?

- » What did you learn about how giving can affect one's spiritual growth?

- » How might your experiences this week affect how you interact with God regarding giving in the future?

- » What would you like to ask God for as you consider going forward from here?

End the discussion with prayer.

WEEK 12
Free To Partner With God

For God is the one who provides seed for the farmer and then bread to eat. In the same way, he will provide and increase your resources and then produce a great harvest of generosity in you.

2 Corinthians 9:10 (NLT)

The Lesson 15 minutes

Listen to the podcast for Week 12. It further examines Paul's words to the Corinthian church regarding giving. We are also given four practices to help us continue to grow in financial freedom with God.

Real Life Practice 15-30 minutes

Answer the questions below to help determine what practices will help you going forward in your journey into financial freedom.

> In spiritual self-evaluation, the intention is to come honestly and humbly before God. However, you may also experience guilt or shame at not measuring up. Whatever you discover, remember that nothing can separate you from the love of God in Christ Jesus. Allow this truth to enfold and dissolve any feelings or thoughts that would keep you from God's loving presence.

Read this portion from the Scripture passage:

Remember this—a farmer who plants only a few seeds will get a small crop. But the one who plants generously will get a generous crop. You must each decide in your heart how much to give. And don't give reluctantly or in response to pressure. "For God loves a person who gives cheerfully." And God will generously provide all you need. Then you will always have everything you need and plenty left over to share with others. As the Scriptures say,

*"They share freely and give generously to the poor.
  Their good deeds will be remembered forever."*

For God is the one who provides seed for the farmer and then bread to eat. In the same way, he will provide and increase your resources and then produce a great harvest of generosity in you.

Yes, you will be enriched in every way so that you can always be generous. And when we take your gifts to those who need them, they will thank God. So two good things will result from this ministry of giving—the needs of the believers in Jerusalem will be met, and they will joyfully express their thanks to God.

As a result of your ministry, they will give glory to God. For your generosity to them and to all believers will prove that you are obedient to the Good News of Christ. And they will pray for you with deep affection because of the overflowing grace God has given to you. Thank God for this gift too wonderful for words!

2 Corinthians 9:6-15 (NLT)

1. A Final Evaluation

Review again your overall financial situation; refer to your survey from Week 2. Note the current state of your money—income, savings, and debt—and all your possessions. Also reexamine your general giving habits from Week 11. Keep all of this in mind as you work through the exercises below.

On each of the following 10 point scales, rate your engagement in these practices.

1. When I make decisions regarding money and possessions, ***I become aware of my emotions before acting.*** I evaluate my internal motivations in prayer with God and ask Him to reveal if I am being compelled by anything other than love, joy, peace, patience, kindness, goodness, faithfulness, gentleness, and self-control (Galatians 5:22-23).

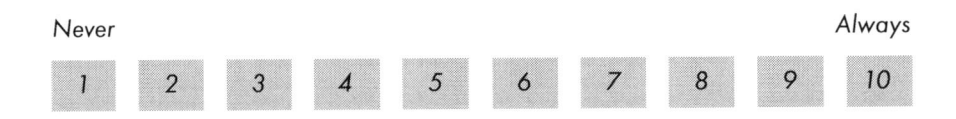

Never | 1 | 2 | 3 | 4 | 5 | 6 | 7 | 8 | 9 | 10 | Always

✎ What leads you to rate yourself in this way?

✎ If you engaged in this practice more often, what difference do you think that could have in your life?

2. When I make financial plans, ***I purposely invite God's input and perspective.*** I do this through a relational, honest conversation with God about my intentions, leaving space for Him to communicate directly with me through His word and in prayer.

   Never   Always
   | 1 | 2 | 3 | 4 | 5 | 6 | 7 | 8 | 9 | 10 |

   ✎ What leads you to rate yourself in this way?

   ✎ If you engaged in this practice more often, what difference do you think that could have in your life?

3. I draw my financial conclusions *in light of who God reveals Himself to be.* I compare my assumptions about money and possessions against God's character and His promises in His word. If I find I hold perspectives that are ungodly, I bring them repentantly to God in prayer and invite Him to change my heart and mind.

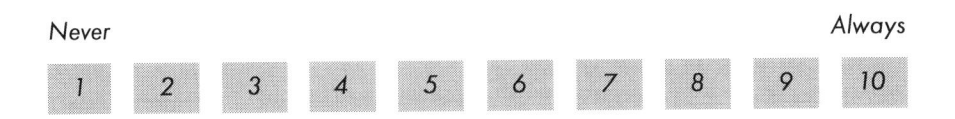

Never *Always*

| 1 | 2 | 3 | 4 | 5 | 6 | 7 | 8 | 9 | 10 |

✎ What leads you to rate yourself in this way?

✎ If you engaged in this practice more often, what difference do you think that could have in your life?

4. Once I come to a financial decision and take action, ***I release the ultimate outcome to God,*** trusting Him to do with His resources whatever He likes. I accept God's will over my own and remember that His actions can have effects in His kingdom beyond my grasp or understanding.

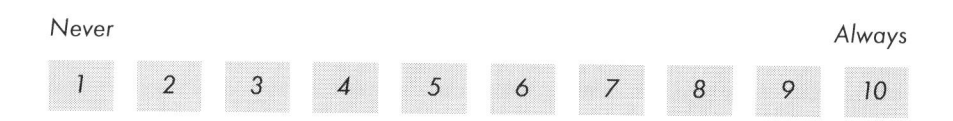

Never | 1 | 2 | 3 | 4 | 5 | 6 | 7 | 8 | 9 | 10 | Always

✎ What leads you to rate yourself in this way?

✎ If you engaged in this practice more often, what difference do you think that could have in your life?

✎ Which of these four practices would you like to most grow in? Why?

2. Sharing And Receiving From God

Talk to God about what you have learned about yourself from the exercise above.

Share with Him what you would like your relationship with Him to be like—particularly around financial issues—going forward from here.

End your prayer by spending a few minutes sitting quietly in God's presence. Simply receive His love for you.

OBSERVATION NOTES 5-10 MINUTES

Spend a few minutes answering the following questions based on your experiences with the Real Life Practice.

Refer to the word chart below when answering.

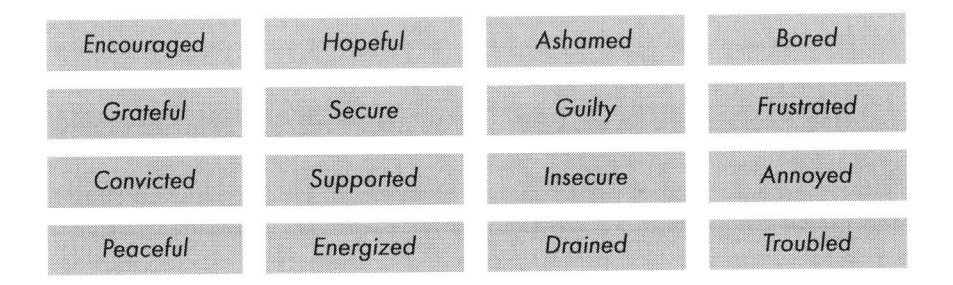

Encouraged	Hopeful	Ashamed	Bored
Grateful	Secure	Guilty	Frustrated
Convicted	Supported	Insecure	Annoyed
Peaceful	Energized	Drained	Troubled

✎ How would you describe your experience evaluating yourself against the four practices for financial freedom? What thoughts and feelings arose in you as you rated yourself and answered the questions?

- What did you discover about how you might want to relate to money and possessions going forward from here?

- How might engaging more in these practices of financial freedom affect your relationship with God?

- How might engaging more in these practices of financial freedom affect your relationship with others in your life, such as your family, your friends, your church, your work, the world?

Reflection

15-20 minutes

Find a quiet place to answer the questions below. Begin by reading the Scripture passage for this week.

I really don't need to write to you about this ministry of giving for the believers in Jerusalem. For I know how eager you are to help, and I have been boasting to the churches in Macedonia that you in Greece were ready to send an offering a year ago. In fact, it was your enthusiasm that stirred up many of the Macedonian believers to begin giving.

But I am sending these brothers to be sure you really are ready, as I have been telling them, and that your money is all collected. I don't want to be wrong in my boasting about you. We would be embarrassed—not to mention your own embarrassment—if some Macedonian believers came with me and found that you weren't ready after all I had told them! So I thought I should send these brothers ahead of me to make sure the gift you promised is ready. But I want it to be a willing gift, not one given grudgingly.

Remember this—a farmer who plants only a few seeds will get a small crop. But the one who plants generously will get a generous crop. You must each decide in your heart how much to give. And don't give reluctantly or in response to pressure. "For God loves a person who gives cheerfully." And God will generously provide all you need. Then you will always have everything you need and plenty left over to share with others. As the Scriptures say,

*"They share freely and give generously to the poor.
    Their good deeds will be remembered forever."*

For God is the one who provides seed for the farmer and then bread to eat. In the same way, he will provide and increase your resources and then produce a great harvest of generosity in you.

Yes, you will be enriched in every way so that you can always be generous. And when we take your gifts to those who need them, they will thank God. So two good things will result from this ministry of giving—the needs of the believers in Jerusalem will be met, and they will joyfully express their thanks to God.

As a result of your ministry, they will give glory to God. For your generosity to them and to all believers will prove that you are obedient to the Good News of Christ. And they will pray for you with deep affection because of the overflowing grace God has given to you. Thank God for this gift too wonderful for words!

2 Corinthians 9:1-15 (NLT)

✎ What thoughts and feelings do you have as you read Paul's words to the Corinthian church regarding their financial giving and the spiritual effects of their gift?

✎ What difference do you think it makes whether someone gives a gift for God's kingdom grudgingly, reluctantly or in response to pressure, as opposed to giving it freely and cheerfully?

- What might happen (or not happen) if someone were to make a financial plan without including God's perspective in the process?

- How might remembering God's character and love towards you and others affect what you do with your money and possessions?

- How might releasing the outcome of your financial decisions to God increase your trust in Him?

✏ How have this week's exercises deepened your understanding of the passage?

GROUP DISCUSSION
30-60 MINUTES

Use the questions below to guide your group discussion. This week, we pondered Paul's words in 2 Corinthians 9:1-15. Refer to the teachings and your experiences as you share together.

Read 2 Corinthians 9:1-15 aloud.

- » What did you learn from the Scripture passage?

- » What did you discover about yourself as you looked at the four practices for financial freedom?

- » How might your experiences this week affect how you deal with money and possessions in the future?

- » Looking back over the entire study, what have you learned about financial freedom and how to gain it?

- » What would you like to ask God for as you consider going forward from here?

End the discussion with prayer.

Going On From Here

> *We've recorded a short podcast to help you transition the concepts that you learned in No Strings into your day-to-day life. You'll find it on the podcast page of our website.*

Now that you've completed *No Strings*, where do you go from here? You will likely want to keep engaging in the practices that have been helpful during this study. In order to assist you in going forward, we have compiled some exercises and prayers to help you continue to process and grow in your capacity to include God in your financial affairs.

We suggest, as you look through these options, that you ask God to lead you in choosing what may be of benefit to you. Also, think about limiting the number of practices or prayers that you try at one time. This will allow you to give your full focus to the activity and reflect on how it is affecting your life and relationships.

The following activities are categorized by themes that were covered in the study:

» On Remembering God's Generosity And Love, page 153
   A nightly or weekly prayer

» On Including God In Your Financial Decisions, page 154
   A monthly financial review with God

- » On Evaluating Your Giving, page 156
  A monthly practice, and when needed

- » In Times Of Financial Stress, Anxiety, Or Crisis, page 158
  A prayer in times of need

- » On Taking Stock Of Your Possessions, page 160
  An annual practice

On Remembering God's Generosity And Love

A nightly or weekly prayer

Our financial freedom is dependent on the degree that we believe in God's generosity and love for us as individuals and as a church. If you struggle to recognize or accept God's care for you, this prayer can help you be more observant of His provision in your daily life.

Prayer To Remember God's Generosity And Love

> *What then shall we say to these things? If God is for us, who can be against us? He who did not spare his own Son but gave him up for us all, how will he not also with him graciously give us all things?*
>
> Romans 8:31-32

In the evening take a few minutes to review your day.

- » Ask God to remind you of any times during the day when He demonstrated His provision for you. Sit quietly as you notice what comes to your mind.

- » As you think on these circumstances, do you remember feeling God's love for you? Can you feel it now?

- » Now ask God to help you remember any times during the day when you felt like you needed to provide for yourself. What influenced these times of independence?

- » Slowly read the verses above from Romans 8. Let the words ruminate through your mind and heart. What does God want you to remember as you leave this time of prayer?

ON INCLUDING GOD IN YOUR FINANCIAL DECISIONS

A monthly financial review with God

We want to become practiced at talking with God about each of our financial decisions. One way to begin to engage with God around money is to include a time of prayer once a month when you pay your bills, set your budget, or reconcile your finances. This regular rhythm of prayer and reflection will help you to grow in attachment to God.

> *Not that I am speaking of being in need, for I have learned in whatever situation I am to be content. I know how to be brought low, and I know how to abound. In any and every circumstance, I have learned the secret of facing plenty and hunger, abundance and need. I can do all things through him who strengthens me.*
>
> Philippians 4:11-13

Gather whatever financial papers that you need for your monthly task: bills, budget, checkbook, computer, etc. When you are settled, begin by inviting God into the process. Acknowledge that He is with you and is the supplier of all of your needs.

» As you look over your income, notice any emotions that emerge in your heart. Talk with God about whatever you feel.

» As you look over your expenses, again notice any feelings that you become aware of. Express these emotions to God.

» As you assess your financial situation, do you feel that you have too many resources, not enough or just the right amount? Evaluate your level of contentment with the amount that you possess.

» Are there any needs that you want to bring before God? Tell Him what you desire and ask for His perspective. What is God asking you to trust Him for?

» Is there anything about your income or expenses that God is inviting you to change?

- » What are you thankful for? How do you want to express your gratitude to God in this moment?

- » As you complete your task, take a moment to release the outcome of your monthly expenditures to God.

On Evaluating Your Giving

A monthly practice, and when needed

Giving is a spiritual practice that can affect our relationship with God and others. By taking time once a month to review your regular giving with God, you can give focused attention to this important practice in your life. Likewise, when you are presented with new opportunities to contribute, you can use this practice to discern together with God what actions you should take.

Practice Reviewing Your Giving With God

But who am I, and what is my people, that we should be able thus to offer willingly? For all things come from you, and of your own have we given you.
1 Chronicles 29:14

» Become aware of God's presence with you.

   Ask God to lead and guide you through this survey.

» Review your charitable gifts from the last month.

   Note to whom you have given and for what amounts.

   Tally up all that you have given.

» Become aware of your emotions.

   How are you feeling towards those you have given to or are considering giving to?

   Note if your motivations are driven by love, joy, and peace, or by pride, obligation, guilt, shame, or discomfort.

   Talk with God about your motivations.

» Consider equality in God's kingdom.

Note the level of need compared with your provision.

Consider if you're giving a lot, an average amount or not enough, for each gift and overall.

» Ask God for His perspective.

Ask God if He thinks you are giving too much, too little or just enough, for each gift and overall.

Consider if God is inviting you to change the recipients of your giving in some way.

Consider if God is inviting you to alter the amount of your giving in some way.

» Make a plan with God.

If you discern an invitation from God, write out what those changes would be, along with how and when you will make them.

Ask God to keep you aware of His presence as you carry out your plan.

» Take action and release the outcome to God.

Offer your plan to God.

Thank God for providing you with the opportunity to share in His kingdom work.

Express your desire to increase your faith in His action in the kingdom and the world.

In Times Of Financial Stress, Anxiety, Or Crisis

A prayer in times of need

We will all inevitably face times of financial stress or crisis. These times may be brief or prolonged seasons in our lives. During these difficult circumstances, it is wise to include intentional times of prayer to ensure that we are exercising our trust in God as our Provider and Shepherd.

Begin your prayer time by taking a few deep breaths. Notice where your body is tense. Try to relax any muscles that are tight or stressed. Breathe deeply. Acknowledge that God is with you. If it is helpful, light a candle to represent God's presence.

Read the following verses:

> *Let your reasonableness be known to everyone. The Lord is at hand; do not be anxious about anything, but in everything by prayer and supplication with thanksgiving let your requests be made known to God. And the peace of God, which surpasses all understanding, will guard your hearts and your minds in Christ Jesus.*
>
> Philippians 4:5-7

- » Assess your emotional state with God. Ask Him to help you recognize any feelings of worry, anxiety, fretting or despair that you may be feeling. Take a moment to accept these feelings and to acknowledge them before God.

- » As you think about the circumstances that are bringing up these feelings, what do you want to tell God? Is there anything you want to ask Him for? Additionally, is there someone that God wants you to tell about your need? Take a moment to ask God and to listen for a response.

- » If you are experiencing anxiety, ask God to remind you of how He has provided for you in the past. Spend some time thanking Him for His faithfulness.

- » Now, ask God to show you any ways that He is working in the midst of this situation. Thank Him for whatever He reveals.

- As you release these cares into God's hands, ask that He replace your fears and anxieties with a sense of His peace.

- End by reading again the verses from Philippians 4.

On Taking Stock Of Your Possessions

An annual practice

It is important to be aware of what we have so that we can make wise choices with God about our finances and possessions. As days pass, it is easy to overlook what we have accumulated. This annual practice will help you become more mindful of what God has put in your care.

Make an Intention to Practice

Mark an annual date on your calendar to spend time working through this exercise. Choose a date of renewal, such as the first of the year, a birthday or a time of spring cleaning.

Practice Reviewing Your Possessions With God

> *Both riches and honor come from you, and you rule over all.*
> *1 Chronicles 29:12a*

- » Focus on God.

    Ask God to make you aware of His presence with you as you engage in this practice.

- » Review your finances.

    Estimate what is in your checking, savings, investments, retirement accounts, etc. Include any currency on hand. Note any debt.

- » Review your major possessions.

    Write down any major items that you own: property, modes of transportation, businesses, recreational equipment, etc.

- » Review the rest of your possessions.

    Walk around your house/apartment/etc. and note your possessions.

Open up drawers, cupboards and closets.

Include any additional items out of sight, such as in an attic, shed, garage or storage unit.

» Note your emotional reactions.

Would you say that you have a lot, an average amount or not enough?

Do you wish you had more, wish you had less or are you content with what you have?

» Ask God for His perspective.

Ask God if He thinks you have too much, too little or just enough.

Consider if God is inviting you to alter the amount of what you have in some way.

» Make a plan with God.

If you discern an invitation from God, write out what those changes would be, along with how and when you will make them.

Offer your plan to God

Ask God to keep you aware of His presence as you carry out your plan.

» Practice thanksgiving and faith.

Thank God for His provision for you.

Express your desire to increase your faith in His provision.

Reflections for Christians in Leadership

After completing the personal projects and reflection questions for each week, spend some time in prayer considering these additional questions regarding your leadership role.

> *To help you get started with these questions, listen to the podcast "A Message for Leaders" on our website.*

Week 1 – Getting Started

- As you explore your personal attachments and assumptions regarding money, are you willing to let God show you how these might be affecting your organizational responsibilities?

✏ What is your reaction to the idea of talking with God about your leadership position and the money you are responsible for? Excited? Concerned? Intimidated? Weary? Cautious? Write down your thoughts and feelings.

✏ In light of your answers above, can you offer yourself to God and accept whatever He may want to reveal to you through this study? What would you like to say to Him?

Week 2 – Seeking Financial Freedom

✏ Note all of your organizational fiscal responsibilities. Include both monetary and physical assets under your control. Generally, how much are you responsible for?

✏ How much time and energy do you think you give to tending to, growing and/or stewarding your organization's finances?

✏ How attached do you feel to these financial responsibilities? If they were to shrink or be taken away, how do you think you would react?

Week 3 – God Is A Giver

✎ You've looked at how you personally accept and receive God's love and care. Are there any differences in how you look for, accept and receive God's provision for your organization?

✎ Do you talk with God about your organization's financial needs and/or surpluses? If so, what do you share with God?

✎ When your organization is in need, do you usually include God in how you handle the situation? If so, what does that process look like? If not, what could that process look like?

Week 4 – Acknowledging Our History With Money

✏ How would you describe your organization's history with money?

✏ What would your colleagues say is your reputation in your organization's fiscal affairs? Ask someone and see if their answer matches your own assessment.

✏ Now sit with Jesus and talk with Him about your role in your organization's financial history and reputation. What might He have to say about how you contribute to it or how you could help change it?

Week 5 – Our History With God And Money

✏︎ Think of a time when you took an important financial action for your organization without including God in your decision-making process? What specific instance comes to mind? What were you trying to accomplish? How did that decision turn out?

✏︎ Did this financial action bring you closer in relationship to God or further away? How so?

✏︎ As you consider that decision and its ramifications, what might your actions reveal to you about how much you do or don't want God to be involved in the financial life of your organization? What difference do you think His presence might make?

Week 6 – What Is Our Current Identity?

- Consider your organization's current financial situation. What does its fiscal condition communicate to you about the kind of leader you are?

- What if your organization's financial resources suddenly increased by 50% or more? What is your initial reaction to imagining that situation? What would you hope this financial increase would tell you about the kind of leader you are? What do you fear it might communicate to you?

- What if circumstances suddenly reduced your organization's finances by 50% or more? What is your initial reaction to imagining that situation? What would you hope this financial decrease would tell you about the kind of leader you are? What do you fear it might communicate to you?

Week 7 – Using Money To Create A Reputation

- ✏︎ What would you like your organization's financial reputation to be? Within your organization? Among similar organizations or competitors? Within society?

- ✏︎ What do you display or what actions do you take in order to convey to others your organization's fiscal position? Are any of these things a stretch to make happen? Have any of them started to feel like a burden to maintain?

- ✏︎ Is there some aspect of your organizational financial dealings that you would feel uncomfortable or embarrassed if other people knew about? What are you afraid would happen if other people knew about what you're keeping hidden? What do you expect would change in their estimation of you and your organization?

Week 8 – In God We Trust

🖉 What organizational fiscal responsibilities do you tend to feel anxious about? How do you usually try to calm your anxiety about these things?

🖉 If God invited you to entrust the provision of your organization to Him, what would that specifically mean to you and how you execute your financial responsibilities?

🖉 How could you become an advocate for trusting God and His provision within your organizational culture?

Week 9 – Trusting God Together

✏ Have you ever thought of other organizations as your competition for limited resources? Where does that thinking lead you?

✏ If you work in a Christian environment, what might be different if you were to consider other Christian organizations as your allies in God's kingdom work? How might that change the way you relate with other Christian organizations?

✏ If you work for a secular company, how do you think Kingdom values should influence the way you view other organizations in your industry?

✏ Spend some time talking with God. Ask Him to make you aware of a social or market need that you could help meet by partnering with another organization, rather than "competing" with them.

Week 10 – Contentment: A Sign Of Freedom

- As you consider your fiscal responsibilities for your organization, what are you most attached to? Is there a particular group, project, product, department, or initiative that you are personally invested in making successful? Talk with Jesus about your feelings and desires for this area. Tell Him honestly what you would like to have happen.

- If Jesus were to allow to happen what you desire, how would that affect your relationship with Him in your role as a leader? If Jesus were to allow the opposite of what you desire, how would that affect your relationship with Him in your role as a leader?

- If whatever Jesus allowed to happen in this area came out of His love for you and for the people involved in this area, would you be willing to let go of your desires for this attachment and allow Jesus to handle it however He pleases? How would that affect how you engage in this area as a leader?

Week 11 – Free To Choose

- How do you communicate with others about the potential financial resources that they could give to or invest in your organization? Are you ever tempted to use guilt, shame, status, obligation, or stretching the truth as a motivator for receiving money from others? How does that affect how you think and feel towards these people? How do you suppose it affects how they think of your organization?

- How might it look to be like Paul in 2 Corinthians 8, encouraging others to participate with you out of joyful eagerness and love? Is there a way to offer them the opportunity to partner with you for the good of God's kingdom and for their own spiritual growth?

- If you were to change how you communicate to others about their participation, how might that affect your personal relationship with God as a leader of your organization?

Week 12 – Free To Partner With God

On each of the following 10 point scales, rate your engagement in these practices as an organizational leader with financial responsibilities.

» When I make financial decisions for my organization, ***I become aware of my emotions before acting.*** I evaluate my internal motivations in prayer with God and ask Him to reveal if I am being compelled by anything other than love, joy, peace, patience, kindness, goodness, faithfulness, gentleness, and self-control (Galatians 5:22-23).

Never / Always

1 2 3 4 5 6 7 8 9 10

» When I make financial plans for my organization, ***I purposely invite God's input and perspective.*** I do this through a relational, honest conversation with God about my intentions, leaving space for Him to communicate directly with me through His word and in prayer.

Never / Always

1 2 3 4 5 6 7 8 9 10

» For my organization, ***I draw my financial conclusions in light of who God reveals Himself to be.*** I compare my assumptions about money and possessions against God's character and His promises in His word. If I find I hold perspectives that are ungodly, I bring them repentantly to God in prayer and invite Him to change my heart and mind.

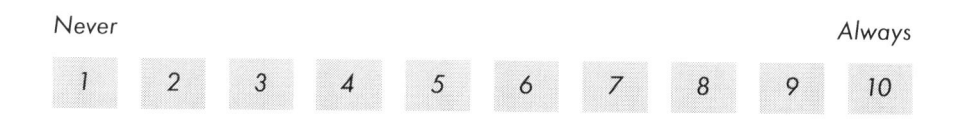

Never / Always

1 2 3 4 5 6 7 8 9 10

» Once I come to a financial decision and take action, ***I release the ultimate outcome to God,*** trusting Him to do with His resources whatever He likes. I accept God's will for my organization over my own and remember that His actions can have effects in His kingdom beyond my grasp or understanding.

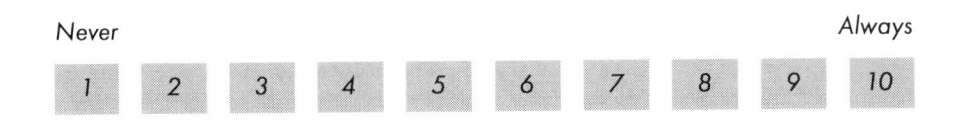

Never / Always

| 1 | 2 | 3 | 4 | 5 | 6 | 7 | 8 | 9 | 10 |

✎ If you engaged in these practices more often, what difference do you think they could have in your organization?

Talk to God about what you have learned from the exercise above. Share with Him what you would like your relationship with Him as an organizational leader to be like going forward from here.

About Grafted Life

Authors

Debbie Swindoll

Debbie is the founder of Grafted Life Ministries. She serves as the producer and teacher of Grafted Life's formation and training products. Debbie writes, speaks, and consults on issues of relational theology and spiritual leadership. She also ministers as a spiritual director for both individuals and groups. Debbie received her Master of Arts in Spiritual Formation and Soul Care from Talbot School of Theology, Biola University in 2007.

Building strong relationships with God and others has become the passion of Debbie's life. She and Curt have been married since 1981 and love spending time with their adult children and growing grand-babies.

Monica Romig Green

Monica works in Content Development for Grafted Life Ministries. With Debbie, she has co-written most of Grafted Life's materials. She specializes in creating interactive prayer exercises and small group experiences. Monica has been offering spiritual direction since 2003 and was the founding director of the Evangelical Spiritual Directors Association (ESDA), a ministry of Grafted Life. With degrees from Stanford University and Talbot School of Theology, Monica combines her background in theatrical improvisation with her spiritual direction work to offer her creative Pray Thru Play retreats across North America.

Monica's husband Matthew is a scholar, teacher and writer on spiritual growth, emotion and neuroscience. Together, they enjoy many nerdy pastimes, such as playing vintage pinball and video games, reading humor books, and visiting weird roadside attractions.

Consultant

Curt Swindoll

Curt Swindoll is the executive vice president for strategy at Pursuant, a fundraising agency in Dallas, TX. His career has spanned six industry sectors (Manufacturing, Technology, Banking, Nonprofit, Professional Services, and Energy), serving in or consulting functional areas as diverse as operations, sales and business development, marketing and branding, IT and software development, fundraising, consulting and board development, strategic planning, finance, client service and support, and P/R and corporate communications.

In 2000, Curt received an MBA from Pepperdine University. He regularly speaks and writes on business, leadership and fundraising issues and practices.

Free Online Resources

Through our website, individuals and churches can access:

- *guided reflections for connecting with God in daily life*
- *articles on topics pertinent to relational/spiritual growth*
- *prayer exercises that practice Christian living*
- *book reviews and recommendations*

In addition we produce *The Invitation: A Daily Pause for Your Soul*, a free morning reflection written by Debbie Swindoll, delivered to your email inbox. *The Invitation* serves both Christian leaders and lay persons for their continued spiritual and relational growth.

Small Group Resources

Life with God: A Journey of Relationship

Life with God is a Bible-focused, small-group process designed to move the things Christians know about God from their heads into their daily lives. Heart transformation happens when *Life with God* groups experience and connect with God's presence, love, and care. These thoughtful discipleship studies help participants understand how God uses life circumstances to invite us into conversations about His will and our hearts.

Through six 12-week semesters, Christian small groups learn to care about what is most important to God: a loving relationship with Him, with themselves, and with others. New converts and seasoned saints alike will discover a fresh approach to leaving their old ways behind and entering into God's abundant life.

Known By Love

Known By Love is a 12-week interactive journey designed to get you involved in your current Christian relationships. This experiential study breaks down the theory of love into small relational concepts and skills that can be digested and applied in community with others. Through Scripture meditations, guided relational projects, personal reflections and group questions, this study carries a Christ-like love into real life encounters.

Do You Love Me? Group Study

This four week group experience explores the biblical foundation for relationship with God and one another. It is rich in personal illustration and invites individual reflection, practical application, and honest group discussion.

The Art of Spiritual Leadership

This six week peer training is designed for any Christian leader, regardless of their ministry context or experience, and prepares them to cultivate small group communities that are spiritually focused and skillfully loving.

Spiritual Direction Resources

Evangelical Spiritual Directors Association (ESDA) is an international association and the largest online directory of evangelical Christian spiritual directors.

Spiritual direction is a confidential one-on-one session with a trained spiritual director that explores how God is working in and through your life. Sessions may be arranged in-person, over the phone, or online. Hospitable and grounded in biblical truth, spiritual direction can help you grow in prayer and live into your calling as a follower of Christ.

ESDA member spiritual directors are a trustworthy resource to pastors and lay persons: formally trained listeners who ascribe to an ethical code and an evangelical creed. ESDA provides professional support to member spiritual directors as well as a platform for promotion and access to the ministry of spiritual direction in evangelical environments.

Made in the USA
San Bernardino, CA
28 August 2016